Rome

To judge from current descriptions – both in the media and from the people who live there – Rome is a city close to collapse. Every year it slides a little further down the liveability rankings. As well as the issues faced by all major capitals – hit-and-run tourism, traffic, the gap between the neglected suburbs and a liberal, Airbnb-dominated centre – in recent years Rome seems to have been determined to add a string of abominations all its own: a series of disastrous administrations, ubiquitous corruption, fascist resurgences that have entered the mainstream, widespread criminality and mafia activity – an apparently irredeemable situation that was symbolised perfectly by the city's world record for the spontaneous combustion of its buses. But this narrative of destruction seems to be contradicted by just as many signs pointing in the opposite direction. The first surprise is the absence of the sort of mass exodus we would normally expect: an overwhelming majority of Romans would never dream, not even for a second, of 'betraying' their city, and the many new arrivals who have settled here in recent decades are often indistinguishable from the natives in their attitudes and profound love for this 'sticky city' that 'clings to you with its predilections and its flaws'. Look closely and you will discover Rome's ability to reconcile countless contradictions and opposites. It is an 'incredibly deceptive city' that 'always appears to be something it is not' and is what it appears not to be. We think of it as big, but it is, in fact, immense, Europe's most sprawling metropolis. Its limits extend way beyond the terminal stops of its metro lines and far beyond the Grande Raccordo Anulare, its ring road, Italy's longest urban motorway, which encloses only a fraction of the city. But above all, debunking the most misleading stereotype of all, despite being founded over 2,770 years ago, Rome is a profoundly modern city, like 92 per cent of its buildings, and anything but 'eternal', given that its growth since the end of the Second World War has 'wiped out vestiges of millennia and upset the geography of half the surrounding region'. So if we want to understand Rome and solve its problems – or, at least, try to do so – we should think of it as an ordinary city. Only unique.

Contents

The photographs in this issue were taken by photojournalist and portrait photographer **Andrea Boccalini**. He began his career in Guatemala on projects focusing on child labour and rural resistance movements. Following on from his journalism he developed a passion for portraiture, which, along with his love of jazz, led to collaborations with some of the biggest stars in the global jazz scene. His work has been published in magazines and newspapers such as *The New York Times*, *The New York Post*, *La Repubblica*, *JazzTimes* and *Rolling Stone*. He has spent many years charting the stories of people on the margins, the dignity of those who live on the edges of our cities and the fringes of society. He also works in advertising, with campaigns for the likes of Huawei and Lavazza and was Leica's first ambassador in Italy. He has worked with the MAXXI Foundation and was a consultant for three seasons of Sky's *Master of Photography* series.

Rome in Numbers

POPULATION BEFORE AND AFTER THE UNIFICATION OF ITALY

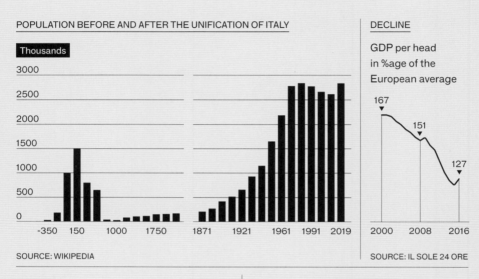

SOURCE: WIKIPEDIA

SOURCE: WIKIPEDIA

DECLINE

GDP per head in %age of the European average

167
151
127

2000　2008　2016

SOURCE: IL SOLE 24 ORE

GREEN CITY

82K hectares out of a total of 129K hectares of the Metropolitan City of Rome, 68.3%, are green spaces

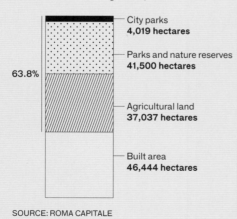

City parks
4,019 hectares

Parks and nature reserves
41,500 hectares

63.8%

Agricultural land
37,037 hectares

Built area
46,444 hectares

SOURCE: ROMA CAPITALE

SORRY, THE TRAFFIC WAS TERRIBLE

Average number of hours per driver lost to traffic jams annually

Bogotá	191
Rio de Janeiro	190
Rome	**166**
Paris	165
Belo Horizonte	160
Mexico City	158
Dublin	154
Istanbul	153
São Paolo	152

SOURCE: INRIX

CAR OWNERSHIP

A survey of 1,000 inhabitants
aged 18–54 in each city

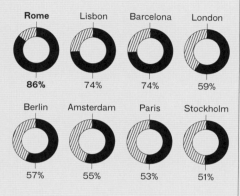

Rome	Lisbon	Barcelona	London
86%	74%	74%	59%

Berlin	Amsterdam	Paris	Stockholm
57%	55%	53%	51%

86% of Romans own a car, and 60%
more than one; 94% would like to see
traffic reduced.

SOURCE: ORB INTERNATIONAL

ALL ROADS LEAD ...

Most common names
of roads and squares
in Italy

**Roma
7,870 municipalities**

Giuseppe Garibaldi
5,472 municipalities

Guglielmo Marconi
4,872 municipalities

Giuseppe Mazzini
3,994 municipalities

Dante Alighieri
3,793 municipalities

SOURCE: TOR VERGATA
UNIVERSITY OF ROME

THE 8TH KING
OF ROME

250

goals scored
by Francesco Totti
in Serie A (all
in an A.S. Roma
shirt), second only
to Silvio Piola.

FANS

Other
18.3%

Roma
50.1%

Lazio
31.6%

SOURCE: WILLIAM HILL

SORRY, THERE WERE NO TRAINS

 Population (millions)

↑ Total length of the metro system (km)

Urban area (km²) →

SOURCE: ARSENA ARCHITETTURA

SORRY, THE BUS
CAUGHT FIRE

Fires on ATAC
and TPL units

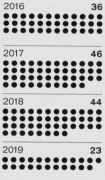

2016 — 36
2017 — 46
2018 — 44
2019 — 23

SOURCE: IL MESSAGGERO

The Not So Eternal City

MARCO D'ERAMO
Translated by Oonagh Stransky

Villa of the Quintili on the Via Appia Antica.

With no entrepreneurial tradition of any note, the Italian capital is still held prisoner by forces that keep its development in check: a bureaucratic apparatus with a culture of welfare dependency, a clan of developers operating outside the law and a cuckoo in the nest, the Vatican, which owns a quarter of the city's real estate. And then there's the damage caused by tourism, which has led to the depopulation of the city centre with a side-order of rampant gentrification.

9

Rome is an incredibly deceptive city: it always appears to be something it is not. It seems to be ancient but is actually modern; it seems never to change, yet in fifty years it wiped out vestiges of millennia and upset the geography of half the surrounding region. That Rome is deceptive is inscribed in its best-known sobriquet, the Eternal City. In reality, although it was founded 2,770 years ago (according to the myth of Romulus and Remus), 92 per cent of the city is not just modern but contemporary, as much the product of massive recent immigration as Chicago or Manchester were in their day. If in the time of its empire Rome was the largest metropolis on earth, peaking at 1.5 million inhabitants in the 2nd century CE, by the late medieval period it had shrunk to a town of no more than 30,000 inhabitants. By about 1600 the population had crept back up to some 110,000, settling at around 170,000 in the following centuries. When Piedmontese troops stormed the city in 1870, putting an end to the Vatican state – which by then had 200,000 inhabitants – Rome was just the fourth largest city in Italy after Milan, Naples and Genoa.

In newly unified Italy the biggish town to which *Roma caput mundi* had been reduced was repopulated with civil servants from the north and labourers from the south and the Apennines, hired as masons on new construction sites or as domestic servants for petit-bourgeois white-collar households. There followed a steady growth for about a century, and in 1950, for the first time in almost two thousand years, the city returned to the population levels of antiquity. In 1971, precisely one hundred years after the unification of Italy, it peaked at 2.8 million inhabitants.

The demographic boom after the Second World War coincided with an economic boom. So, too, the stagnation of its population in the past thirty years coincided with the economic stagnation into which Italy sank after the end of the Cold War. During the Cold War the American empire reserved special treatment for its marches: they had to be 'success stories', windows for showcasing Western capitalism. Economic growth was also needed to neutralise the strength of the left in some of these frontline countries, so there was an Italian boom and a Japanese miracle that in many ways ran in parallel during the Cold War.

During this period Italy could do anything it wanted: go into debt (no one seemed to pay much heed), unleash inflation and resort to devaluation, collude with the Mafia (Christian Democracy depended on it in Sicily) and pursue an anomalous path of state capitalism. In the post-war years, the anomaly of the 'Italian case' in matters of property was glaring, particularly in Rome. To begin with, unlike in other European countries, in Italy there was never any serious attempt at public housing. According to the Italian Institute of National Statistics, in 2015 the housing stock of the public housing

MARCO D'ERAMO is an Italian journalist and writer. He took physics at university, later studying sociology with Pierre Bourdieu at the École Pratique des Hautes Études in Paris. He has worked for *Paese Sera*, *Mondoperaio* and *il manifesto* and has written for a number of newspapers, including *Internazionale*, *MicroMega*, *New Left Review* and *Die Tageszeitung*. His books translated into English include *The Pig and the Skyscraper: Chicago – A History of Our Future* (Verso, 2003) and his recent study of global tourism, *The World in a Selfie: An Inquiry into the Tourist Age* (Verso, 2021). His most recent work, *Dominio* (Feltrinelli, 2020), is a history of the class struggle.

'Throughout the modern history of Rome, the *palazzinari* have ignored any and all zoning regulations, planning restrictions and building limitations.'

institution (IACP) constitutes only 2.7 per cent of the total, while housing cooperatives or socialised housing accounts for a mere 1 per cent. Moreover, the contribution of the state has shrunk over time: currently, new public housing amounts to just 0.5 per cent of construction under way. In a country where public spending accounts for about half of GDP, not only has the state left a key area of its economy and society completely in the hands of private interests but it has allowed total deregulation of this market.

*

As Rome grew from one to almost three million inhabitants, the utter absence of the state in this area found expression in a phenomenon virtually unknown in other countries – in fact, no word for it even exists in French, English or German – but which in Italy is a massive, chronic structural reality: *abusivismo*, a term that requires no adjective to specify what kind of abuse is involved. What it designates is every kind of illegal construction activity, conducted without a permit and/or in violation of regulations, by-laws, safety rules, often indeed without so much as an appearance in a land register. These range from such minor infractions as enclosing a balcony to create or extend a room, raising the roof of a pre-existing building by one or two floors or putting up a shack on the outskirts, to erecting huge industrial warehouses and creating entire neighbourhoods of ten-storey apartment blocks.

Abusivismo in Rome has two key components and phases. The first involves migration – a construction worker moves to the city from the countryside and builds his own home after hours and in secret. This component was significant in the first phase of the city's demographic expansion and can be defined as an '*abusivismo* of necessity', given the complete inability of the state to provide affordable housing for a rapidly growing population. Tens of thousands of immigrants came to the capital each year and had literally to camp out in *borgate* and *borghetti* (two further untranslatable terms) in tin shacks without running water, plumbing, sewage or electricity. (A somewhat folkloric but essentially accurate portrayal of what the world of the Roman *borgate* was like can be seen in the film *Brutti, sporchi e cattivi*, which won Ettore Scola the award for best director at Cannes in 1976.)

The second component of *abusivismo*, long present but dominant since demographic expansion tapered off and the population of Rome began to contract, is property speculation by developers large and small known as *palazzinari*, a third term that is largely untranslatable. Throughout the modern history of Rome, often with the tacit complicity – if not outright agreement – of its municipal authorities, including those of the left, *palazzinari* have ignored any and all zoning regulations, planning restrictions and building limitations. As Paolo Berdini (who served as an urban planner for the Five Star-led city council for seven months in 2016) writes in the appendix to the fifteenth edition of Italo Insolera's classic work on the modern urban history of Rome, *Roma moderna: Da Napoleone I al XXI secolo* (Einaudi, 2011): 'Rome holds the title of the capital of Italian *abusivismo*, both because Romans invented and have tolerated it since the 1920s and 1930s, and because Rome has in absolute terms the largest number of neighbourhoods that are *abusivi* … In total, these newly approved illegal areas extend for more than 100 square kilometres, while the entire built surface of Rome covers some 500 square kilometres. In other words, 20 per cent of the capital of Italy is completely *abusivo*.'

*

There is a close link between *abusivismo* and fiscal evasion, and not simply because no one pays taxes on their illicit constructions or the incomes they yield but also because these two forms of illegality constitute the most important sources of an underground economy, which is abnormally large in Italy – reckoned to be 20 or even 30 per cent of GDP. Another factor is that both are taken to be structural features of the Italian landscape, alterable by neither governments nor parties, including those of the left. The logical consequence is that both tax evasion and illegal construction are periodically condoned on payment of a relatively insignificant fine, with the excuse that the state needs the cash to alleviate its financial woes. Each such amnesty offers further opportunities and encouragement for tax evasion and *abusivismo*, since tax evaders and illegal builders know that one day their crime will be commuted with a simple fine. The successive pardons, moreover, result in a heavy net loss for the state, which has to supply all the infrastructure (electricity, gas, running water, sewage, roads) for the illegally built neighbourhoods: the public authorities end up spending five times as much as

they take from the fines they collect. It is no accident that two out of three of the amnesties for *abusivismo* and three out of the six for tax evasion were issued under the premiership of Silvio Berlusconi, who propagated the slogan 'Everyone master in their own home' and incited Italians on his television channels not to pay their taxes.

For an example of the fervid legislative fantasy of Italians and their republic's ambiguous relationship with legality, one need look no further than the imaginative device included in the amnesty of 1985, which exists nowhere else in the world: the rule of silent assent. When more than four million requests for commutation came in, local governments were overwhelmed and could not decide which infractions should be pardoned. So, with luxuriant Italic ingenuity, a law was passed in 1990 stipulating that so long as a decision was not made, 'silence by the administration in question is equivalent to acceptance of the request'. In other words, if a citizen requests a pardon from the state and the state does not reply, the citizen can consider himself pardoned. On the island of Ischia, for example, accommodating a total of 21,817 resident families, 24,000 requests for commutation of *abusivismo* were submitted, the majority of which still have not been processed.

In the political geography of the post-war period the Roman *borgate,* characterised by massive illegal building practices, were always a bulwark of the Italian Communist Party (PCI), although there were few factory workers in Rome – it has been argued that under fascism and during the long reign of the Christian Democrats the capital was deliberately never industrialised to ensure there was no class conflict near government ministries and the palaces of power. By way of

THE PASSENGER   Marco D'Eramo

The Basilica of Maxentius.

compensation, construction came to be the most important industry in the city, as it remains today. Building workers were often to be found in the ranks of the PCI alongside railwaymen and other proletarian categories in the public sector.

*

Beginning in 1968 and for several years thereafter, the most combative forces in popular struggles in Rome came from the inhabitants of these low-income settlements. In Rome the *borgate* put in the first red municipal council – a coalition of the PCI, the Italian Socialist Party (PSI) and the Italian Democratic Socialist Party (PSDI) – which, in turn, nominated a leading art historian, Giulio Carlo Argan, as mayor.

The left held office in Rome from 1976 until 1985, but the balance sheet of those years was modest. True, the job the left faced was immense, and some problems were tackled energetically: shacks were demolished, the suburbs received services and sewers and Line A of the metro was inaugurated. Two specialised city offices were created: one for upgrading the *borgate*, the other for restoration of the city's historic centre. A new impulse to public building came with the inauguration of the Corviale (a single structure comprising 1,200 flats) and the construction of Tor Bella Monaca, uplifted from an illegal *borgata* to a popular neighbourhood with services, infrastructure and new high-rise towers before falling into decay in the following decades.

In effect, however, rather than combating *abusivismo*, the left chose to try to fix its detritus and clean up the neighbourhoods it had created. As Italo Insolera wrote in *Roma moderna*: '"Do well what others have done poorly" ended up becoming the philosophy of the left council, instead of doing other things and creating a different city.' Later, when it returned to office between 1993 and 2017, the watchword became even more minimalist: 'Do less badly what others have done miserably.'

Over this long period the regularisation of the *borgate*, giving the *borgatari* access to ownership of their dwellings, revolutionised the political geography of Rome. If the centre of the city had historically voted for the right – the neo-fascists of the Italian Social Movement (MSI) and the Italian Liberal Party (PLI) – or the Christian Democrats and their allies, while the *borgate* and outskirts voted for the left, workers transformed into homeowners shifted politically towards the right, while the unemployed and marginalised proletariat and sub-proletariat of the city abandoned the *n*th avatar of the former PCI for Beppe Grillo's Five Star Movement. The Democratic Party (the current label for what was once the Communist Party) now finds its supporters in rich neighbourhoods. In their relations with building speculation, Roman administrations on the left, first under Argan and then under Luigi Petroselli, at first negotiated an 'honourable surrender' to property speculation, then collaborated with it and, finally, became subaltern accomplices of it.

*

Rome is, let us not forget, dominated by four main powers: Italy's public administration, the Catholic Church, the real-estate industry and the tourist industry, because of the city's enormous heritage. The relation of the municipality of Rome to the government is that of a beggar, always beating its chest and pleading for alms to pay off its debts and finance good works. But the austerity does not allow the state to be as open-handed as in the past. These days Rome is the capital of a country that is a state in free-fall and is deindustrialising: productivity is declining; conservative estimates reckon the cost of corruption at €60 billion ($70 billion) a year and that of tax evasion at another €90 billion ($105 billion). For the first time since the war the life expectancy of Italians is not lengthening but shortening.

This country and this state cannot and do not want to be as generous as in the past, which is one of the reasons – setting aside some of the shady characters around Virginia Raggi, mayor of Rome since 2016 – why the freshly arrived Five Star Movement has confronted a kind of 'mission impossible', tasked with the repair of a city where nothing works and burdened with a debt of €17 billion ($20 billion, nearly $7,000 per inhabitant).

True, the city of Rome has always been in debt. In the 1960s its debt was already 1.5 trillion lire, which would be €18 billion ($21 billion) today, close to the current figure, but back then there was no pathology of debt, so much so that the Olympics held in Rome in 1960 were – along with those of Mexico City in 1968 and Seoul in 1988 – games of which no one has ever known the cost. Since austerity arrived, begging the state to help with the running costs of the city gets short shrift, and mendicancy is activated ever more by 'major events' like the football World Cup (1990), the World Swimming Championships (2009) or Holy Years (like the various Jubilees of 1966, 1975, 1983–4, 2000, 2015–16).

Throughout the world major events – and sporting events in particular – have always been and continue to be the best of all opportunities for making a fortune through mega-corruption. The advantage that such events have over other major construction projects is that they are, precisely, events – that is, they have an insurmountable deadline: everything has to be ready by the referee's whistle or the opening ceremony. This kind of deadline not merely allows but renders inevitable corruption on a scale unthinkable in other kinds of construction. Everyone knows that there is corruption not only, and not even mainly, when stadiums and the rest are put out to tender (if they are at all) but above all when initial cost estimates are revised upwards. It is revisions – which cause the final price tag to rise like dough – that create the largest corrupt profits. After winning its bid with a rock-bottom offer, a company will then 'discover' during the course of its works indispensable 'variances' that increase the final cost tenfold. The incredible advantage of sporting events is that contractors can always delay the works by just the right amount to get any price increase they want, with the argument that 'there's no time' – no time to give the job to someone else, no time to scrutinise the variances, no time to revise the estimates and so on. Everything must be completed by the deadline, literally 'at any cost'. It is enough to think of the 1990 World Cup in Rome, a disaster symbolised by what was supposed to be a terminal for Fiumicino Airport next to the railway stop at Ostiense, which

cost 350 billion lire (equivalent to $415 million today) before it was abandoned and became a refuge for the homeless. In 2012 it was snapped up by Oscar Farinetti – a prominent backer of Matteo Renzi, who was prime minister from 2014 to 2016 – for Italy's largest chain of upmarket food stores, Eataly.

*

We could talk endlessly about corruption. Perhaps one day we should ask ourselves why in living memory not a single struggle against it has ever had a left outcome, the upshot invariably favouring the right. One explanation may be that every campaign against corruption leads to a demand that economic transactions be wrested from the sphere of politics and restored to the sphere of the economy – which is to say, to capital. But the true problem of Italian corruption is that elsewhere people are corrupted to do things, while in Italy people are corrupted *not* to do them. In Spain scandals erupt one after the other, but a network of high-speed trains was built. The city of Madrid has twelve subway lines; Rome has two and a half. Barcelona is much less opulent than Milan, but it, too, has twelve underground lines where Milan has five. In Italy public works have biblical lifespans, allowing costs to levitate to the heavens.

In Rome, work on Line B of the subway had begun in the 1930s to connect Termini railway station to the new district around the Esposizione Universale di Roma 1942, which was supposed to have been a model fascist city (the World Expo was cancelled because of the war). Construction of this line resumed in 1948; the first route was opened in 1955. Most of the stops on it were inaugurated in 1990, and the final extension to the EUR was completed in 2012, sixty-four years later. Meanwhile

The Fonte Laurentina residential
complex, situated just outside the GRA
ring road; thousands of square metres
remain unoccupied.

work on Line A got going in 1964.
Inaugurated by Petroselli in 1980, the
final section was opened only in 2000
– thirty-six years later. Line C, which is
supposed to pass through the historic
centre of the city, was initiated in 2007
and should have been finished in 2013.
In 2015 the first twenty-one suburban
stations were opened, while the station
next to the Colosseum is slated for 2023
and the others are now up for discussion.
In the meantime, costs have risen from
an original €1.9 billion in 2001 to €2.5
billion ($2.25–3 billion) when the project
was signed, to €3.7 billion ($4.4 billion)
in 2016. Keeping in mind other potential
costs, the final bill could rise to €5.7 billion
($6.75 billion), a cost per kilometre double
that of other European cities. In all, it
will have taken up to twenty-two years to
advance a project that will never actually
be completed.

Rome is proof that harsh laws do not
stop corruption; on the contrary, they
favour it. In theory, the rules that protect
the cultural heritage of Rome are draco-
nian; the Superintendency of Fine Arts can
block any project the moment construction workers come across what Romans
snidely call a *coccio* – a mere shard. A
simple veto by the Superintendency can

prolong projects for decades. That very same body, however, was incompetent (or impotent) in preventing the massacre of the amazing archaeological park of the Via Appia. Unscrupulous millionaires were allowed to build huge villas and swimming pools, defacing and wrecking thousand-year-old ruins. A law that is too severe becomes inapplicable, calling forth an intermediary to soften its edges. Montesquieu once said that he feared a regime in which a judge can show mercy, because in such a land your destiny depends on the whim of the magistrate. In his 2015 novel *Titloi Telous* ('End Titles'), the Greek writer Petros Markaris describes the system of public administration in Greece: the worthiest projects remain mysteriously blocked (because they lack a certificate, a signature, an authorisation, a licence or a topographical map) until someone intervenes, naturally with a kickback, to lift every impediment and let the project proceed.

*

As for the Catholic Church, which governed Rome for some fifteen centuries, it looms so large that it is regularly repressed. If you ask politicians in Rome for some glimpse into the relationship between the city and the Vatican, the answer resembles the way Americans talk about race relations and Indians speak of caste: Vatican, race and caste are problems of the past, which at one point were very serious but which now are 'resolved, or almost'. But from a global standpoint the relevance of Rome consists all but exclusively of the Vatican. The Vatican is the company and Rome is the town, like General Motors and Detroit or Krupp and Essen. Rome is one of those rare cities that hosts two kinds of embassies: every important country has an ambassador to the state of Italy in

Rome and another in the Holy See. The Catholic Church could be regarded as one of the largest multinational corporations in the world, at least in terms of numbers of employees – 1,133,000 (421,000 male and 712,000 female) – with the Vatican operating as the headquarters of a global network stretching across five continents. Thanks to the Lateran Pact signed by Mussolini in 1929, the Catholic Church obtained its own small state (Vatican City, 0.44 square kilometres, 825 inhabitants) with all the privileges of extra-territoriality and a fiscal regime yet more a law unto itself.

No one in Italy can answer the question of how much land the Catholic Church owns. Estimates in newspapers are approximate at best, but it is generally reckoned that a fifth of all Italian real estate is held in the name of the Church; in Italy there are 115,000 ecclesiastic properties, of which nine thousand are schools and four thousand are hospitals and care centres. A quarter of the entire real estate in Rome belongs to the Church. We know for sure that the Sacred Congregation for the Propagation of the Faith (the Propaganda Fide) owns 725 buildings in the city, while the Administration of the Patrimony of the Apostolic See (APSA) possesses 5,050 apartments. Other sources report fifty monasteries, more than five hundred churches, twenty-two convents and four hundred buildings, including houses, seminaries, oratories and about forty colleges. And this patrimony keeps growing; in the city of Rome alone the Church receives approximately eight thousand bequests each year. In Italy almost all approved private healthcare, in large hospitals or clinics, is controlled by the Vatican, and virtually all private education is Catholic.

Until about 1980 the Vatican was a

The Temple of Venus Genetrix beside Via dei Fori Imperiali.

The Not So Eternal City

direct economic agent on the market, active in property speculation, in keeping with a tradition that began with the unification of Italy, when financiers connected to the Church began to sell off some of the vast holdings of the religious orders in the city and its surroundings to profiteers. But then came scandals related to the Vatican Bank (the IOR) and to financiers connected to the Holy See such as Michele Sindona. Since then operations have become more discreet but no less influential. The Vatican preys on the city like a vampire, exacting from it a series of public works and services for which it pays not a penny because of its tax exemption. Furthermore, it receives a good chunk of tourist revenues (a quarter of all private hotels belong to the Church) by renting out empty rooms in convents – empty because of the decline in religious vocations. Rome has 297 convent-hotels, from the House of St Brigid to the Palatine Sisters. Most of these places do not pay normal property taxes, not even a tax for refuse collection. Thus, the Little Helpers of Christ the King – which online says it offers '72 rooms not far from the Basilica of St Peter's with private bathrooms, colour TV, Wi-Fi and an excellent restaurant' – are being sued by the city for €320,000 ($380,000), while the Suore Oblate del Bambino Gesù owes €694,000 ($822,000) in back taxes, and the list goes on.

Among the most pernicious damage the Vatican has inflicted on the city of Rome is the persistence of a papal culture among the public servants who work for the city (it matters little if they come from other regions because everyone 'becomes Roman' pretty quickly). This is a culture of docile servants under an absolute monarchy, the papacy, protest against which was suicide but which, if approached from the right angle, could seem good-natured enough, albeit naturally hypocritical, and which was often distracted and not very meticulous, an assiduous adept of 'keep to your own corner' and 'don't step on my toes, and I won't step on yours'. The result is a public administration pervaded with a kind of lax *omertà*, a code of compromise prefiguring the famous Brezhnevite pact in the Soviet Union: 'They pretend to pay us, and we pretend to work.' This is a culture that leads not only to a generalised corruption but also one that is seeping up from below, starting with the traffic cop who goes into a shop and doesn't pay for his purchases, rising to large-scale theft by big shots with sumptuous expense accounts and ending in kickbacks – Italian has a plethora of synonyms for these, including *bustarelle, mazzette, tangenti, pizzo* – deposited in tax havens abroad. A corpulent, soft mass of inertia, the bureaucratic machine of the city of Rome has proved irreformable, the biggest single obstacle to any attempt at changing daily life in the city.

To this system of 'passive sabotage', public-sector unions have made their own nefarious contribution, transforming defence of workers' rights into tooth-and-nail protection of corporate privileges and absenteeism in a sort of clerico-syndicalism. For example, of Rome's 6,300 city traffic wardens, only three hundred ever work on the streets at any one time, as Ignazio Marino, the independent mayor between 2013 and 2015, complained. In the public bus company (ATAC), the rate of absenteeism is over 15 per cent, more than double that of other transport enterprises. Every day, of its 6,500 drivers at least 970 don't show up for work. In August the percentage rises to more than a fifth. To top it off, there are more than six hundred drivers who have obtained medical

THE PASSENGER   Marco D'Eramo

Workmen in St Peter's Square.

certificates claiming they are unfit to hold a steering-wheel so that they can have a desk job.

*

These viscous dependencies furnished an alibi for the infatuation with Clinton and Blair that swept through the left in Rome in the 1990s. Since the municipal institutions responsible for transport, street cleaning, refuse collection, parks-and-gardens maintenance, cultural affairs and the reception of immigrants had proved inefficient and immovable, the temptation to privatise them was strong,

handing their management over to coop-eratives, possibly belonging to the left. Here on full display was the naivety, if not outright blindness, of the personnel of the Italian left, aghast when it discovered that the cooperatives in question were working closely with a fascist crook at the head of the Roman *malavita* in the scandal that became known as the Mafia Capitale (see the sidebar on page 54). In point of fact, the figures involved in this affair were pittances (some tens of millions of euros) compared with those at stake in the city's large-scale building or transport projects – for example, the €6 billion ($7 billion) being sunk in the metro's Line C.

Across these years one of the updrafts of the breeze from Clinton and Blair was the enthusiasm with which local authorities (and the municipality of Rome in particular) invested in derivatives, swaps and other exotic packages, both on the stock market and over the counter (in the same way that Goldman Sachs acted as a debt consultant to the Greek state). Plain here, too, was the thrill of the parvenu who feels he has entered the *salotto buono* of the elite and can compete on equal terms with the wizards of world finance. So, in construction projects, the left showed the same excessive confidence that it could govern forces stronger than itself. Such faith exuded from the very name of its first urban programme – a 'Plan for Certainties', no less. This was a scheme that included a conceptual novelty of the bureaucratic imagination, in the form of a mechanism dubbed 'urban compensation', which works like this. If a developer is forbidden to build x number of square metres in one area of the city (because of landscaping regulations, archaeological or other restrictions) they can be 'compensated' with permission to build in another area, and if land values in this area are lower, the square metres allowed are increased: doubled or perhaps even trebled. The first time this arrangement was applied, a developer denied permission to build 1.8 million cubic metres in Tor Marancia, near an archaeological park, was compensated with five million cubic metres beyond the Grande Raccordo Anulare (GRA; see the sidebar on page 129), the ring road around the city, sixty-eight kilometres long and officially equivalent to the M25 around London, although that is nearly three times its length).

In practice, the principle of compensation had a perverse and unforeseen effect. Developers were prompted to build ever further from the centre of Rome and beyond the GRA. The city council tried to ennoble the resulting eyesores by talking of 'new centralities' that would become 'edge cities', defined as suburbs that have developed their political, economic and commercial base independently of the centre of a city. Giving a new name to the concrete toadstools proliferating around the GRA did nothing to change their nature, however; no company wanted to move into these desolate areas, the buildings designated as offices remaining empty, unsold and unrented. After a while the developers went back to the city authorities for permission to convert what they had erected from office to residential use. The 'new centrality' became another example of Orwellian Newspeak, these areas reverting to typical dormitory cities equipped at best with vast commercial centres – the years of rule by the left saw an explosion of shopping malls. In the next five years, when the city was in the hands of the right (2008–13), the trend only worsened. At national level the Berlusconi government in one of its final acts approved a housing plan that allowed *federalismo demaniale,* 'federalisation of public property', or its transfer from the state to local authorities. On the first list 17,400 buildings passed to municipalities, which promptly put them up for sale to raise cash. As Paolo Berdini writes in *Breve storia dell'abusivismo* ('A Brief History of *Abusivismo*'): 'So the law on the alienation of public assets is a kind of instigation to delinquency: municipalities are forced to sell precious valuables to maintain essential services.' And in order to raise yet more money they are forced to permit more construction, more concrete.

The upshot of all this has been devastating: the city that seems the same as ever to tourists has in reality been transformed into a dismal sprawl across an enormous area. The city of Rome is the largest municipality in Europe, with a total area of 1,287 square kilometres, of which 550 square kilometres are built on; the historic centre accounts for a mere fifteen square kilometres – one fortieth of the total. A trip around the urban spread makes for a horrific journey: the sprawl has made any kind of public transport impossible, since population density is so low it becomes economically unviable. Rome has one of the worst car-to-inhabitant ratios in Europe. There are seventy-one cars and 13.7 motorcycles and scooters – in all nearly eighty-five motorised vehicles – for every one hundred inhabitants; children, the elderly and the infirm included.

*

The dilation of this hinterland highlights another paradox. While the population of Rome stagnates new construction proceeds frenetically, yet the number of families who can't find homes also continues to grow. The disconnection cannot be explained just by the contraction in the size of the nuclear family (a trend throughout the West), such that a population whose numbers remain the same divides up into more units that need more housing. There are between 200,000 and 250,000 empty apartments in Rome but just as many citizens who can't find housing, for property markets abandoned to *laissez-faire* lack any rationality. What is missing in Rome is housing at reasonable prices for the young and for immigrants. The *palazzinari* build apartments few can afford: supply does not meet demand. Meanwhile, new buildings, even if empty, function as collateral for further bank loans for developers to embark on further building projects. Satellite cities continue to mushroom despite the financial crisis, amid a complete surrender of the left to property speculation. The parabola of two

BLESSED REVENUES

The Church knows that material wellbeing does not lead to happiness – which is perhaps why the Vatican anticipated the debates questioning the validity of economic indicators and is the only state that does not measure its GDP. Nor has it managed to get around to publishing a financial statement: the accounts for the Curia – in other words, just the administrative section, roughly a third of the total workforce – were presented in 2020 after four years of silence. But this does not mean the Vatican has no economy. The bulk of its revenues come from its property holdings and, to a lesser extent, its financial portfolio. Then there are donations from the faithful and state funding, such as the 'eight-per-thousand' contribution made by Italian taxpayers that is divided between organised religions and state projects (the website www.icostidellachiesa.it estimates the value of public funds and exemptions enjoyed by the Church). But there are also commercial activities, such as the Vatican Museums. More surprising is the contribution from the four retail outlets theoretically reserved for the Curia, residents and secular staff (roughly 3,600 people): a petrol station, a pharmacy, a tobacconist's and a supermarket. According to a 2015 investigation carried out by Emiliano Fittipaldi, they bring in $130.2 million a year, more than the museums and the Pontifical Villas combined. Part of this is explained by the market for collectable postage stamps, but there is more. Medicines sold at a discount or that cannot be found elsewhere attract almost two thousand customers to the pharmacy every day, while cigarettes, alcohol and fuel are tax free. If these really were just for the clergy they would all be smoking an average of three packs a day! According to a 2012 study cited by Fittipaldi, the Vatican has the highest consumption of wine anywhere in the world, another figure that does not appear to be a valid indicator of wellbeing.

Walter Veltroni
2001–8

Gianni Alemanno
2008–13

After a thirty-year political career in the communist PCI and socialist PDS, during which he served as deputy prime minister and minister for cultural and environmental heritage (as well as editor-in-chief of the left-wing newspaper *l'Unità*), Veltroni was elected mayor for the first time in 2001 and re-elected five years later. He resigned in 2008, not even halfway through his second term, to campaign in the national election (in which he suffered a defeat). During his seven years in office the development masterplan was approved (the day before his resignation), with the aim of 'repairing' the outskirts and the centre with the creation of 'new centralities'. The new Auditorium was also inaugurated as a part of a major focus on culture, with initiatives like the 'White Nights' arts festivals, major free concerts and trips for Roman schools to countries in Africa as well as to Auschwitz. The city experienced a tourism boom fuelled by the Catholic Church's Great Jubilee in 2000. In a recent book on the city (*Roma: Storie per ritrovare la mia città*; Rizzoli, 2019), Veltroni writes that during those years 'there was a "climate" of openness and tolerance, a spirit of solidarity and welcome, that no one in good faith could fail to remember'. Negative opinions of his time in office focus on the eventually abandoned plan for an underground car park at the Pincio and a significant increase in debt, which was criticised by his successor, due in large part to dubious financial operations such as the 'City of Rome' maxi-bond issued in 2004.

Following the interim administration under extraordinary commissioner Mario Morcone after Veltroni's resignation, the mayoral elections were won by Gianni Alemanno, the candidate for the newly established Popolo della Libertà (People of Liberty) coalition. While he had been a member of the far-right MSI from a very young age and was arrested three times for assault and violence in the 1980s, although always acquitted, he renounced extremist views when he became one of the co-founders of the MSI's successor party, the National Alliance (AN). His electoral campaign was based on issues of public safety and urban decline. Once he became mayor he appointed an extraordinary commissioner for immigration, requested and obtained three hundred soldiers to protect the neighbourhoods and stations on the outskirts of Rome, armed the traffic police and dismantled six traveller camps following a census. In response to the controversy over remarks defending the country's fascist past, he gave his approval for the Shoah Museum, inaugurated in 2015. Towards the end of his term approval was given for Rome's special metropolitan-city status as Roma Capitale, giving the city – and its mayor – more autonomy and greater jurisdiction in the light of its role as the Italian capital and the location of diplomatic delegations. He was defeated in the 2013 elections and spent the following years in court following accusations of external cooperation in a mafia association (later dismissed), aggravated corruption and illicit funding as part of the Mafia Capitale investigation, leading to a six-year sentence, upheld on appeal.

Ignazio Marino
2013–15

Virginia Raggi
2016–21

With a background as a surgeon specialising in organ transplants, Marino was elected three times to the Senate, in 2006 as an independent on the Democrats of the Left (DS) list then in 2008 and 2013 with the centre-left Democratic Party (PD). He also chaired the parliamentary commission to investigate the effectiveness of the national health service but resigned from all his positions to stand in the 2013 elections. During his short term in office he made as many enemies as he launched initiatives, as his plans fell foul of the city's established interests: the closure of the Malagrotta landfill site, the ban on snack trucks in the city centre (a monopoly of powerful criminal families), the closure of the Imperial Fora and Piazza di Spagna to traffic (against the wishes of traders), the demolition of illegal constructions barring access to Ostia beach, the opening of new Line-C metro stations and even the recognition of foreign gay marriages, which earned him the hostility of the Vatican. In 2014 the Mafia Capitale investigation erupted: Marino personally came out clean, but his council did not (and previous administrations even less so). A series of scandals that attracted significant media attention – in particular the 'receipts affair', which challenged the legitimacy of certain entertainment expenses paid for on the municipal credit card – led to him tendering his resignation. In 2016 the court of Rome absolved him of all accusations of embezzlement and fraud.

After six months of interim administration Rome elected Virginia Raggi, a lawyer and member of the anti-establishment Five Star Movement, as the city's first female mayor. Her campaign promises were to fight corruption and withdraw the city's candidature for the 2024 Olympics, a decision she announced three months after her investiture. During her term the (pre-existing) issues with public transport and waste disposal have intensified: each year more than twenty buses owned by the public-transport provider ATAC catch fire through poor maintenance and overuse. In 2018 there was also a fire at the Salario mechanical-biological treatment plant, which handled a quarter of the capital's waste. Along with the drop in recycling collections the blaze reintensified Rome's waste-management emergency. The mayor was investigated for abuse of authority in relation to the appointment of staff in her office (but later absolved) and as part of a probe into the construction of the new A.S. Roma stadium in Tor di Valle (case dismissed). In a survey published by the newspaper *Il Sole 24 Ore* in 2020 Raggi occupied the penultimate position in the ranking of Italian mayors by approval ratings. In the summer of the same year she announced she would stand for another term in the 2021 elections, even though this was not allowed under her party's internal regulations (which were subsequently amended).

The Santiago Calatrava-designed City of Sport, known as the Vela, or Sail, which was due to be completed for the World Swimming Championships in 2009. When it went out to tender the estimated cost was €60 million ($70 million). Even though €240 million ($280 million) has already been spent the complex remains unfinished; to complete the project would take another €400 million ($470 million).

such magnates as Silvio Berlusconi and Donald Trump speaks volumes about the power of the construction sector even in advanced economies.

At municipal level, mayors and town councils in Italy face a multitude of tasks but have only one real power they can use as a resource in performing them, and that is the authority to decide *if* a given piece of land can be built on and *what size* of building can be erected upon it. So inevitably the temptation to make a deal with speculators is strong. When the left ran Rome between 1993 and 2007, however, compromise was gradually transformed into something like complete abdication of responsibility for any kind of urban planning. So much so that the new urban slogan of the period resembled a baroque poem: *pianificar facendo*, 'to plan while doing' – an oxymoron, since one cannot plan what one is in the process of doing. In practice, of course, what *pianificar facendo* meant was being willing to bend to pressure in conceding the fateful 'variances' that are always demanded by contractors. And while administrations have changed over the years, the names of the powerful *palazzinari* are still the same as those who presided over the concrete bonanzas of the 1960s: Caltagirone, Toti, Armellini, Parnasi, Mezzaroma, Cinque, Salini, Caporlingua, Bonifaci, Scarpellini, Navarra.

Let down by the left, which had governed so poorly for so many decades, in 2016 its electoral base swung massively to the Five Star Movement's candidate for mayor, Virginia Raggi. But hope in this change, too, has proved to be in vain. After at first bravely vetoing the nightmare prospect of another Olympic Games in Rome, against intense pressure from the Renzi administration, she caved in to developers set on constructing a vast complex of offices and shopping malls around a new football stadium for the football team A.S. Roma, which she had campaigned against, coming to an agreement with the *palazzinari*. If the predators had proved too strong for the PCI, how could they not devour an improvised and inexpert group like the Five Star council in a single gulp? For its part, while the elephantine bureaucracy of the city resisted left-wing administrations with all the weight of a pachyderm, when it came to the Five Star Movement still more passive sabotage was in order, including refusing to collect rubbish from the streets.

Behind the ongoing paralysis and failure of the Five Star administration, however, lies the long cultural defeat of the Italian left in Rome, which proved incapable not only of projecting a different future for the city but even of managing such changes as were under way. Nowhere is this sad truth clearer than in the field where the Eternal City ought to be unbeatable: tourism.

*

For those who love statistics, Rome has over 2,500 sites of interest and is home to the most monuments of any city in the world, yet the number of tourists from abroad is disappointing, to put it politely. In 2015 international arrivals in Rome were 7.2 million, compared with 17.6 in Paris, 18.6 in London and 11.7 in Istanbul, despite the damage done to Parisian tourism by the terrorist attacks of January and November 2015 that Rome, unlike London, did not profit from at all. Not only that, with an average stay per visitor of 2.3 days, Rome falls far behind the other tourist destinations (6.2 days in London, 6.1 in Paris). Long gone are the days of Goethe, who, when asked 'How long does it take to visit Rome?' replied, 'I have been here for two years, and I still haven't seen it all.' But the worst figure of all is that, unlike London and Paris, few are the tourists who ever return to Rome a second or third time.

In terms of marketing, Rome sells itself badly, partly because it doesn't know how to sell itself and partly because it is a rotten product. Beyond the usual landmarks that you can count on the fingers of one hand – St Peter's, the Colosseum, the Forum, Piazza di Spagna, Piazza Navona – Rome is incapable of arousing the curiosity of the visitor. There are extraordinary places that remain completely unknown, like the volcanic lakes less than twenty kilometres away. There are

> 'The attitude is, let's fleece the tourist. This is a culture of the *sòla* (a rip-off, a setup, a scam).'

jewels off the beaten track of the tourist circuit within the city, like the Basilica of Sant'Agnese outside the walls with its crypt and catacombs, or the extraordinary museum of Montemartini, where classical sculptures are on view in a former thermoelectric plant, complete with enormous turbines of steel and cast iron.

But these places remain reserved for the locals, above all because public transport is a nightmare of inefficiency: during rush hour buses and metro trains resemble those in India, with people pushing their way on board because they pass only 'as often as a pope dies', as they say in Rome. ATAC, the municipal transport company, is €1.3 billion ($1.5 billion) in debt, so its buses are antediluvian, constantly breaking down: every day nine hundred buses out of a total of 1,920 remain garaged; 190,000 repairs are undertaken each year, mainly as a result of damage caused by potholes. The interior of the metro station at the Piazza di Spagna is a dangerous pigsty, right by Via dei Condotti, the Roman equivalent of Rue Faubourg Saint-Honoré in Paris or Regent Street in London. Recycling in Rome is a joke; the city exports its refuse to Germany.

So tourists gather *en masse* along a few streets in the city centre, where restaurants are atrocious (once it was difficult to eat poorly in Rome; now it is hard to eat well) and everything is expensive and inhospitable. Unlike Spain, Italy in general – and Rome in particular – has never developed a tourist culture: the attitude is, let's fleece the tourist as much as we can ('won't be back anyway'). This is a culture of the *sòla* (a rip-off, a setup, a scam) as

they say in Roman dialect. What's more, tourists tend to meet only other tourists because the centre of Rome is empty of all else. In 1950 the inhabitants of the historic centre of town (within the Aurelian walls on the left bank of the Tiber and the Janiculum on the right) numbered 371,000. By 1961 they had fallen to 242,000, by 1971 to 167,000, by 2001 to 111,000 and by 2012 they numbered no more than 85,000. An emptying out is the common end of all touristic cities: once they become so many urban museums they are fated to a long agonising process of embalming. But in Rome this hollowing out is more dramatic than elsewhere because of the economic crisis and rents beyond the reach of the wages of recession.

So the city has divided itself into a minuscule, shabby, historic Disneyland (the Roman Empire, Baroque Rome, etc.) surrounded by a horrid, enormous, fragmented, modern agglomeration in which millions of Romans lead the uncomfortable lives depicted in Andrea Segre's award-winning 2009 documentary *Magari le cose cambiano* ('Maybe Things Change'), which tells the story of the 'new centrality' of Ponte di Nona. But this real Rome remains completely unknown to visitors, just as they also ignore everything that is happening in the arts scene, like the murals of famous street artists on the façades of suburban apartment blocks in Tor Marancia. Then there is MAAM (the acronym for the Museo dell'Altro e dell'Altrove dei Metropoliz) in the eastern suburbs: a former slaughterhouse and pork factory, occupied in 2009 by around sixty homeless families (Ukrainian, Italian, Peruvian and some 'gypsy'), which, as of 2012, hosts important sculptures and paintings in many of its immense spaces, thus making the expulsion of its occupants impossible and putting a spoke in the wheels of one of the largest developers in Rome, Salini Ltd.

Where there are old things, new things are not born; what is new flowers far from the ancient. The trajectory of the city since 1945 has swept away that temporal depth of every space, that stratigraphy of the non-contemporary, which Sigmund Freud in *Das Unbehagen in der Kultur* (*Civilization and Its Discontents*, 1930) could still consider unique to Rome:

What occupies these places today are ruins – but these are not the ruins of the buildings themselves but those of later structures built following fires and destruction ... There is certainly plenty that is ancient buried in the soil of the city or beneath the modern buildings. This is how the past is preserved in such historical sites as Rome. Let us now make the fantastic hypothesis that Rome is not a human settlement but a psychic entity with a similarly long and rich past – that is, an entity in which nothing that once existed has passed away and all the previous phases continue to exist alongside the most recent. In Rome, this would mean that the palaces of the Caesars and the Septizonium of Septimius Severus would still reach their old height on the Palatine and that the Castel Sant'Angelo would still bear on its battlements the beautiful statues that graced it until it was besieged by the Goths, and so on ... Where the Colosseum now stands we could also admire Nero's Golden House; on the piazza of the Pantheon we would find not only the Pantheon we see today, as it was left to us by Hadrian, but, on the same site, the original building erected by Agrippa ... And to evoke one view or the other the observer would perhaps only have to change the direction of their gaze or shift their position.

If Freud could then compare the stratification of the human psyche to the archaeological layers of the city of Rome and the subterranean presence of pre-existent buildings with the hidden memories of childhood, today the visitor can see the stratification of the non-contemporary of which Freud wrote only far from the city centre, out where real human existence proceeds. For example, in Tor Pignattara, five kilometres from the Colosseum, in the middle of the crazed traffic of the Via Prenestina, there is a gravestone from the second century CE. Next to it are fourteen hectares of an abandoned rayon factory that belonged to Snia Viscosa, with rows of buildings in disarray and overgrown wild plants. The owner of the land, a certain Pulcini, wanted to build an underground car park several storeys deep. They tried to dissuade him because deep underneath lay groundwater. The developer went ahead, dug down and so much water came out of the ditch (and what's more it was fizzy, or *acqua bullicante* as they say in dialect) that it created a lake that can be seen on Google Earth (look to the north of Largo Preneste Roma). The lake is now a place for family picnics, neighbourhood parties, children and those who will fight tooth and nail to thwart the undiminished ambitions of the developer. Now and then you see foxes, and wildflowers grow near water pipes, high-rises and the ancient sepulchre. ✒

This article is an abridged version of 'The Not So Eternal City', first published in *New Left Review* 106, July–August 2017.

Roman Soundscapes

Suitcase wheels on the *sampietrini*, water trickling from the *nasoni*, the calls of seagulls, bells striking the hour, the murmuring voices of perambulating priests and nuns – but also the commotion of street fights, the scream of aircraft flying way too low, the horns of the traffic: Letizia Muratori helps us tune into the sounds of her city, a city with its own beautiful and chaotic soundtrack.

LETIZIA MURATORI
Translated by Oonagh Stransky

The Trevi Fountain.

I grew up in a building that looks out on to the Trevi Fountain, so not your average place. In the rankings of Rome's most popular tourist sites, Trevi takes the bronze. Silver goes to St Peter's, while gold is firmly in the hands of the Colosseum. Obviously I'm not talking about the preferences of the sophisticated traveller here, spiritual heir to those on the Grand Tour.

Other than consistently arriving in third place, what does it mean for a child to grow up playing alongside a waterfall, listening to the constant hubbub of tourists? Most of all it means learning about the world through your ears.

As a matter of fact, I don't see Rome – I may never have – so when I moved back to the city after a long time away I knew it had changed from the sounds I could hear.

It struck me early one morning when the noise that awoke me was not the usual refuse-collection truck but the sound of trolley suitcases being dragged along the *sampietrini* cobblestones. Every single building now includes at least one *casa vacanza* or *piccola dimora albergo*. It's hard to say exactly what the latter actually is, but as a creative form of accommodation it seems to have gone over quite well and can usually be identified by two empty amphorae at the front door that are so large they simply can't be missed, not even by someone like me who's oblivious to most visual cues.

The wheeled suitcases come and go at all hours of the day and night, even when the ubiquitous seagulls are silent.

Some numbers: in recent years tourist arrivals in the city have increased by almost 70 per cent, which explains the relentlessness of the clattering wheels on the cobbles. *Ta-tan ta-tan ta-tan ta-tan.* Pause. *Tu-ru-tun tu-ru-tun tu-ru-tun.* If the sound of the wheels on the cobblestones turns into a long continuous hum, with the short *a* turning into one long resonating *u*, it means that the bag-puller has hit the road and is walking along the tramlines, as thousands of tourists have done before him or her.

If it's early morning you can forget about falling back to sleep. Soon enough another one will pass by and then another. If you're not used to the sound you might look out of the window: from up above all you can see is the top of someone's head next to the top of someone else's, both of which are bent over their phones. It's a bit like that old party game of musical chairs: when the music stops you have to freeze. The bag-dragging tourists, caught *in flagrante*, stopping mid-act. They look like statues.

There's something achingly tender about watching two lovebirds leave the city in rapt silence all loaded up with their gear – but the romantic postcard image fades quickly. Soon enough the street-cleaning machines come to brush away the beer, the dregs and the spit from the drunken alleys, their incessant buzz

LETIZIA MURATORI is one of the most original writers on the Italian literary scene, who consistently seeks to communicate contemporaneity through disorientating narrative styles. Muratori's first novel was *Tu non c'entri* (Einaudi, 2005), and since then she has published several novels and short-story collections, including *La casa madre*, *Il giorno dell'indipendenza*, *Sole senza nessuno*, *Animali domestici*, *Spifferi* and *Carissimi*. Over the years her short stories have appeared in such newspapers as *La Repubblica*, *l'Unità* and *Il manifesto*.

Fabrics in a shop selling ecclesiastical clothing
in Borgo Pio, adjacent to the Vatican.

You can't say you've been to Rome if you haven't, at least once, tripped over a *sampietrino* – not the copper coin issued by the Papal States that was in circulation between 1795 and 1801 but those chunks of leucite, an igneous rock typical of the volcanic areas of Lazio, used to pave most of the centre of the Italian capital. While we tend to associate this type of road surface with Rome, only 2 per cent of the capital's streets are actually paved with this material, and you can also find them in many other parts of central Italy. The *sampietrino* dates back to 1725, when Monsignor Sergardi, president of the Fabric of St Peter (the institution responsible for the conservation and maintenance of the basilica), decided to have the streets paved after the carriage carrying Pope Sixtus V almost flipped over in St Peter's Square (hence the name). Since that time the stones have often been used as weapons in disputes between neighbourhoods and during riots and revolts. The laying of these pyramidal, flat-bottomed blocks, also called *selci*, is the job of experts. The individual stones are positioned and then hammered into a bed of sand. The stones are then covered with an even finer-grained sand and lightly dampened with water, and this solution seeps into the gaps and causes the different elements to adhere to even the most irregular surfaces while also allowing for a bit of movement. Unfortunately, the nature of *sampietrini* means that the surface is rarely uniformly flat – cars and buses are particularly noisy on roads paved with them – they require endless maintenance and they're slippery when wet, especially for people in heels but even for those wearing the sensible black shoes favoured by Pope Francis.

sounding like a beehive on wheels. After the brushes comes the lorry that picks up the bottles: restaurant after restaurant, pub after pub, pizzeria after pizzeria, a continuous shattering of glass. As the bins are tipped the bottles knock into each other, lean on each other; for a brief moment it seems like they'll never hit the bottom, and then they crash and it breaks your heart.

Then it's time for the linens. The vans roll in, loading and unloading sheets and tablecloths on to trolleys that make a heinous noise like the grinding of teeth. This, too, is new. Fifteen years ago the only place you'd encounter linen lorries and their henchmen was along Via Veneto and on certain backstreets behind the big hotels. There, you'll find e-scooters now. Even the Lungotevere is full of them. The scooters speed off, feline and panther-like. The problem with them is not the sound they make but the odd posture that their riders are forced to adopt. If you look carefully, it isn't panthers you see but ostriches.

Going back to the subject of rubbish – the principal obsession and cause for complaint for most Roman citizens – some time ago I was telling an American woman about the overflowing bins, and, as usual, I was going on about the sounds connected with them, the noises that certain beasts – gulls and crows mainly – make when nearby. In some areas not far from the centre you can even hear the grunting of wild boars. I must have grunted for emphasis because the woman looked at me as if I was crazy. She hadn't seen any overflowing and neglected bins in Piazza di Spagna – in fact, you don't see them there – only a few concrete receptacles filled with the plastic takeaway containers from salads or spaghetti all'amatriciana or *gelato* cups. And the following day it was

'When night falls on Via del Babuino, the most elegant street in the Tridente, it's so quiet that you not only hear the sound of your steps but also your thoughts, as if they're speaking to you.'

all gone, hosed down. She said that New York City was far dirtier. Or Paris. Rome, especially in the areas around the Tridente – the neighbourhood formed by the three straight roads that extend south from Piazza del Popolo in the shape of a trident that are these days colonised by the big fashion brands in what they consider an open-air showroom – gets washed down every single evening.

When night falls on Via del Babuino, the most elegant street in the Tridente, it's so quiet that you not only hear the sound of your steps but also your thoughts, as if they're speaking to you. Your schizophrenic perambulation is amplified by the hushed ambush of electric cars, taxis that will run you down if you're not careful. But don't worry, accidents rarely happen: you can still honk your horn freely in Rome. And if you don't drive off the second the traffic light turns green you can be sure that someone will remind you to get a move on.

Wild boars aside, 'at night, in Rome, you seem to hear lions roaring'. So wrote Carlo Levi in the famous opening lines of *L'orologio* (*The Watch*). This archaic and powerful vision of the city is often cited by people who complain about the noise pollution produced by other kinds of wild animals: rowdy revellers, the traffic prior to football matches, the noisy procession of tourist coaches along the Lungotevere that dribble urine-like rivulets of condensation as they pass.

Precisely because of my acoustic slant on the city I took Levi's roar very seriously. As someone who is incapable of abstraction, I always thought that beyond the metaphor – whatever it may be – Levi really did hear something in the city at night, something that might have led up to a roar, a situation where a predatory and territorial display would not be out of place. Although it is impossible to reconstruct 'his' lions, I can tell you about my own.

For several years I lived in Prati, a neighbourhood bordered by the courthouse on one side and the Vatican at the other, and about that experience I shall say this: it was not a lot of fun. My flat looked out over a circular piazza where two homeless alcoholics – a couple, man and woman – would often spend the night fighting. She was the boss. She was also very aggressive and often scratched him. He did nothing but whine and complain about his bloody nose. They had a habit of coughing in unison, a chorus of hacking, and those were the only minutes when there was a truce, but after the coughing break they'd jump right back in with their exhausting physical and verbal scuffle. 'You're disgusting,' she'd say, and there'd be the sounds of kicked cans and rolling jars. 'Give it back to me,' he'd sob like a whinging, spoiled brat in a mixture of anger and pity.

One of those nights (which usually concluded with the arrival of an ambulance, because one of them would get

A narrow street in Trastevere.

THE PASSENGER   Letizia Muratori

Fans of the TV series *Fleabag*, with its 'hot priest' interpreted by Andrew Scott, will appreciate this item (and if you haven't yet seen *Fleabag*, put down this copy of *The Passenger* and go and make good the gap in your education). Sales figures reveal that the product in question is favoured variously by the British and American gay communities, priests and nuns in northern Europe and by many of the tourists who visit Rome – it's even on sale at World Youth Day events! That's right, we're talking about one of the capital's all-time best-selling souvenirs, which can be purchased at news-stands throughout the city but can also be ordered online: the 'Roman Priest Calendar'. Developed in 2004 by Venetian photographer Piero Pazzi, the annual calendar depicts twelve handsome young priests and clergymen. Although it is not an official product of the Catholic Church, the calendar is informative: it contains short descriptions of Vatican City, a little papal history from St Peter to the present, information about the Vatican State and a list of works on display at the Vatican Museums as well as other useful stuff, including how to obtain Vatican citizenship and the opening hours and phone number of the chemist's. Even before the more open-minded Pope Francis was elected the calendar had sold a hundred thousand copies worldwide; it's tolerated by the Church because it helps rejuvenate the image of the Holy See. Some of the young men photographed by Pazzi are priests passing through Rome during Holy Week, while others are photographed during religious processions in southern Italy as well as outside the country, especially in Spain, although a number of them responded to an open-casting call to be featured in the beloved calendar.

injured) he started roaring as if he'd just escaped from a cage. 'What're you doing? You idiot!' she said, but you could tell by her surprised, almost piqued, tone that for the first time ever she felt uncomfortable. He may have gone up to her and roared in her face because I heard her shout, 'Don't touch me, you pig of a lion.'

'You pig of a lion' perfectly captures the mind-numbing absurdity of sleepless nights. In Rome you can sleep anywhere as long as there are two of you and you don't mind sharing whatever you have: the piazza, a bottle of wine, a few pieces of cardboard. When they weren't roaring, the couple's voices tended to fade out slowly, tenderly, in an ebb and flow of senseless chatter.

Speaking of chatter, the city of Rome knows no etiquette. Actually, it despises anything to do with it. Back when people were less touchy, before supermarket cashiers started answering your requests with a 'And good morning to you' when you don't bother to greet them warmly (as is the norm in Rome), you never heard anyone say please or thank you at the bar, not even by accident.

The volume of conversations is high, and not just because the centre is plagued by Spanish-speaking religious tour groups. Rome is, of course, a city of churches, too, filled with perambulating priests and nuns, whispering friendly words to each other as they walk, all in perpetual good moods. These polite minuets and chirped amens are the first sign of that world unto itself known as clerical society. Being something of a priestess of dark humour and full of Roman pride and mischievousness, I find priests and nuns can be something of a disappointment. When I see them out for a walk, often near the Pantheon, I can't help but follow

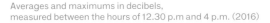

Averages and maximums in decibels,
measured between the hours of 12.30 p.m and 4 p.m. (2016)

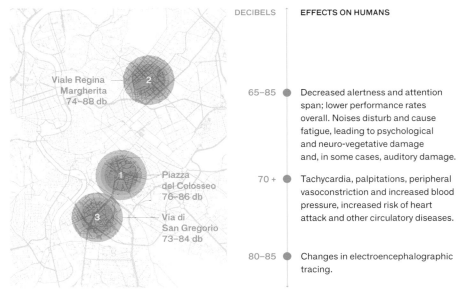

DECIBELS	EFFECTS ON HUMANS
65–85	Decreased alertness and attention span; lower performance rates overall. Noises disturb and cause fatigue, leading to psychological and neuro-vegetative damage and, in some cases, auditory damage.
70 +	Tachycardia, palpitations, peripheral vasoconstriction and increased blood pressure, increased risk of heart attack and other circulatory diseases.
80–85	Changes in electroencephalographic tracing.

Viale Regina Margherita 74–88 db

Piazza del Colosseo 76–86 db

Via di San Gregorio 73–84 db

SOURCE: LEGAMBIENTE LAZIO

them for a bit, hoping that they're headed to one of those historic tailors and dressmakers that have been clothing their kind for centuries. But they never go in. They walk right on by. No one ever stops in front of those majestic shop windows to admire the shimmering candy-coloured outfits reminiscent of Sperlari sweets.

The 'Sperlarisation' of the cassock was a Slavic innovation that we owe to Karol Wojtyła, Pope John Paul II, who, even though he wrapped himself in golden robes, never relinquished his comfy Bata shoes. Ratzinger, meanwhile, brought back ivory, and Francis, as everyone knows, doesn't give a stuff about fashion; he's anti-glitz, anti-aesthetic. I can't tell you how many artisans, silversmiths, turners and cabinetmakers, all of whom have been living off Vatican commissions for generations, now find themselves in a state of ruin. While Bergoglio may be the best-loved pope of recent times and has halted the plummeting popularity of the Church, he's certainly not much liked by the artisans of the old Roman workshops. I can't speak for tailors, though. If you haven't taken your vows, you'll muster up the courage to cross the threshold of one of those shops but once in your lifetime, never to return.

I know because it happened to me a few years ago. I had just had lunch with a writer who believed himself to be God-on-Earth.

'Pope Francis doesn't give a stuff about fashion; he's anti-glitz, anti-aesthetic. I can't tell you how many artisans, silversmiths, turners and cabinetmakers, all of whom have been living off Vatican commissions for generations, now find themselves in a state of ruin.'

God-on-Earth came up with the perfect excuse: 'What does it take? Just tell them that you want to buy a gift for your aunt who's a nun.'

Well, what *does* it take? And then you wonder why people like God-on-Earth are so successful – in some ways they deserve to be.

Let me tell you what it takes. When I pushed open the door a diabolical peal announced my entrance, but no one came out to greet me. I was alone with two mannequins, one in a crimson cassock and the other in Grecian purple. Timidly, as if those two headless horsemen could have booted me out, I approached a glass counter where bits of trim, which looked to me like curtain scraps, had been arranged in anything but a casual manner.

'Interested in a crucicord?' a female voice surprised me from behind.

'No,' I said stepping away quickly and explaining to the saleswoman who sported pairs of glasses in every place imaginable – around her neck, on the bridge of her nose, on her head like a headband – that I wanted to buy a little gift for my aunt, a nun. Right away she pointed through the window to a leather-goods shop down the street. That's where I'd find a bag for her; they had just the thing, sporty little waterproof bags with long straps. Why on earth does nuns' attire always involve inclement weather? It's as if out there, in the real world, on the street, the only thing awaiting them is rain. A priest's wardrobe isn't made up only of anoraks, waterproof ponchos or oilskins – all *sans* hoods, obviously. There's something profoundly sexist about constructing the female religious aesthetic around bad weather that simply escapes me.

Now that I've got that out of my system, and with the saleswoman politely ushering me out of the door, the stubborn rebel in me decided to stand my ground. 'A sweater? A cardigan, perhaps?' I asked. Years of parochial school, for good or ill, didn't leave me completely clueless: nuns need to wear a thin layer of wool, buttoned up to the chin, to protect themselves from the cold.

Result. I walked out of that temple of rules and protocols, the most codified place imaginable, with a loose, cream-coloured, woollen shawl-neck sweater. Adieu, austere mousy greys and dry blue-blacks. With some insistence I had managed to finagle the ideal *weekend garment* for a nun, an exception to the rule that reminded me of those elder statesmen or high dignitaries and lordly officials who are always seen wearing powder-blue cashmere when interviewed at home on a Sunday.

My trophy is safe in my wardrobe, When I reach for it mid-season it rustles noisily. The tissue paper it was wrapped in has an eternal hold on it.

Shifting away from the historic centre, which I don't often do, I can only imagine that the city of Rome – where each municipality is a city within this immense city – produces a quantity of sounds that are in keeping with the vastness of its dispersed grandeur. Despite my best intentions, I couldn't be bothered to go and eavesdrop on each of the zones of the city, and so I can't tell you exactly what kinds of sounds people hear on the Casilina in south-eastern Rome, but I imagine it's entirely different from the rhythms heard in Valle Aurelia in the north-west. Instead, I enlisted the help of a photographer friend who, taken with the obsessive desire to divide and conquer the city, split it up into quadrants and walked them all, allowing herself only brief stretches on a scooter. She never walked fewer than thirty kilometres a day, and I mean never. With astonishing tenacity, she tackled this undertaking during the 'Summer of Covid', marching through barren landscapes in temperatures reaching 40 degrees Celsius, climbing over rusty fences and other obstacles. A slightly built woman who opted to travel light, she took all her photos with her phone. An experienced photographer of architecture, she began in the city centre and worked her way out until she found herself, without even realising it, near a ramp leading to a motorway. Her style is neither street nor classical; impeccability comes naturally to her. She photographs in the same way she irons – and I mean that as a compliment – she gets things done, bends them to her will. Whether shooting an open field worthy of Pasolini or the Pyramid of Cestius, it makes no difference to her.

The result is unsettling. Not only did she succeed where everyone else had failed (or, rather, where no one else had ever tried) by conquering all of Rome, stone by stone, she came out of this dogged enterprise – a record-breaking

feat of endurance, like those people who dance for fifty hours straight – alive and well. Immaculate, even. The images do not betray even a hint of fatigue, nor are they cold. They're pervaded by a passionate desire to possess those forms.

While thanking her for allowing me to cross Rome on foot without taking a single step, I asked her about sounds and noises, if she had noticed any worth mentioning. As I guessed, she listens to music while she walks, a few pop songs on repeat. To be able to focus on the city in front of her she needs a background that leaves no room for surprises. The noises of the city would be as distracting as an ever-changing playlist. So while walking from Via Fosso della Magliana to the Corviale and from the Corviale to the Casetta Mattei (around eight kilometres in total), she listened to the Counting Crows track 'Mr Jones' – *sha la la la la la hey la*, etc. – non-stop.

Her phone died only once, while she was at Ciampino Airport, and there she had to use earplugs because of the noise of the aeroplanes. Despite the pandemic and a general reduction in flights, a few planes were still taking off.

People who live in that area are victims of brutal noise pollution. In the past fifteen years low-cost flights landing at Ciampino have quadrupled. The data speaks for itself: when a Boeing 737 takes off it registers 105.5 decibels on Via Girasole, 102.4 on Via Potenza, 97.7 in the

MONUMENTAL TREES

Rome, by some measurements, is the European city with the highest percentage of public green space in Europe, and yet public awareness of this great heritage is scant. Antimo Palumbo, a writer and tree historian, has taken on the task of cataloguing the city's trees and of conferring the title of 'most monumental tree'. This title does not necessarily go to the oldest tree in the city, something that can often only be estimated, as in the case of the cork tree at the Botanical Gardens on the Janiculum that is apparently more than six hundred years old. The famous cypress tree in the Baths of Diocletian has origins that are more legendary than historical: it is said to have been planted by Michelangelo in 1562. The dating of the twin palms in the Roman Forum – which, at thirty metres in height, reach way above the rooftops – is also impossible. As a matter of fact, Rome has only forty-five officially recognised living monuments (more than half of which are located in Castel Porziano) out of a tree population of 300,000. Often even the most famous trees in Rome remain a well-kept secret and are never reported, surviving and blending in with their neglected surroundings. Sometimes the trees die in anonymity after living for five hundred years, as in the case in 2018 of the Quercia del Lupo, the holm oak in Villa Borghese. From a historical perspective, Palumbo distinguishes eight different eras of Rome's trees: ancient Roman (native specimens such as holm oaks, evergreen oaks and other imported trees such as plane trees, pines and pomegranates); medieval (trees that grow spontaneously and were used for timber and for their fruit); Renaissance (trees that can be linked to the birth of the Renaissance-style villa and the importing of plants from other continents); Papal (a fondness for elms and mulberry trees); French (trees that can be found in public parks such as the Pincio and in a great many varieties); Piedmontese (which include hybrid plane trees and palms); fascist (Italian trees: pines, holm oaks and laurel); and post-war (plants and trees sidelined by streets and buildings).

park on Via Sauro. The maximum legal limit for residential areas is sixty-five.

People living in Ciampino and Marino, the areas worst affected by take-offs, were grateful for lockdown, but the noise associated with landings is no joke either, and the reach is even wider. Planes can be heard coming in as far away as Quadraro, Capannelle, Osteria del Curato and Parco degli Acquedotti, sections of the city with tens of thousands of inhabitants.

I used to like the sound of planes in the same way that I like church bells, but when I think about the people living in Ciampino my passion for aviation doesn't feel quite so harmless.

My friend the photographer, the conqueror of Rome and reliability incarnate, called me back to tell me something you'd only notice if you're not from here. Other than the sounds of planes, when she wasn't listening to music she was struck by the widespread din, from Piazza del Popolo to Fonte Meravigliosa. Humans make a huge amount of noise in Rome, even when simply walking down the street.

Going back to church bells, we hear them a lot in Trastevere. Every now and then they ring for the dead. Also in Trastevere, every day at noon you hear the sound of cannon being fired from the Janiculum. There's the noise of the Carabinieri returning on horseback to the barracks at San Michele. There's the ungainly screeching of the parakeets that have invaded the Botanical Gardens. There's the rowdy, frat-party shenanigans of the students. (With two American universities in the area, Trastevere has become something of a campus.) When a bus slams on its brakes along Lungotevere Sanzio it sounds like the trumpeting of an elephant, which would be almost funny if it weren't so

deadly. In the middle of August, with Romans away on vacation, it's so quiet you can hear the sound of water flowing from the drinking fountains, interrupted only by a periodic and exaggerated sneeze. People from Trastevere sneeze in a theatrical, almost ancient way. Trastevere is the den where the sounds of the city are born, live and die.

'I wouldn't live in that vaudevillian part of town if you paid me,' a rather idiosyncratic friend commented about Trastevere when I asked him for his thoughts on nocturnal noises in residential neighbourhoods.

For years this friend has been devoted to guerrilla gardening, traversing stretches of northern and north-eastern Rome by bike. And what exactly is guerrilla gardening, you ask? I'll let him explain.

'It's a response to the breakdown in the parks-and-gardens services after years of staff cuts, lack of funding and lack of equipment. The contractors who win the tenders offered by the city either decide to scrimp or take advantage of loopholes or abandon the bids they've won while waiting for even more lax contracts.'

'But what's the whole guerrilla thing about? What exactly do you do?' I ask.

'Let's start with the tree-lined streets.'

'Sounds like a good place to start.'

'First we salvage the trees that are in a state of neglect by carefully selecting cuttings that can be transplanted. I'm talking about plants such as oleanders, privets, plane trees. Then we replant them and provide them with supports and braces, protective nets, we water them and we clean out the tree pits or whatever they're called. Anyway, you get the idea.'

'Not exactly, but that doesn't matter. Go on.'

'One of the most common problems

'When it's not surprising us with new invasive sounds, the city makes itself heard through barking, cawing, grunting and roaring, through conversations on the streets and the ringing of bells.'

we encounter is that the shoots that grow up next to old stumps that haven't been removed tend to grow out of balance when the wood in the dead trunk deteriorates; parks-and-gardens services don't bother taking care of them, but those of us who care about all living things are willing to take the risk.'

'And how exactly is a transplant carried out?'

'The following equipment is what's needed for guerrilla gardening. Write this down: a hoe, a pair of gloves, a 1.5-litre bottle of water to wet the soil, a protective net to cover the young plant, a bamboo brace (usually forty-to-sixty centimetres in height) and, of course, some two- or three-year-old saplings. Sometimes, albeit rarely, we tie a tag to the brace with instructions.'

'While you're guerrilla gardening, do any particular noises come to your attention? Have you noticed anything new recently?'

'I tend to focus on the sound of my recently lubricated bike chain.'

'Nothing else? No nocturnal animals?'

'Over at Villa Ada there's a mysterious bird that caws mechanically like the one with crystal feathers in that film by Dario Argento. And there are other kinds of horrifying things out there at night, too.'

'Terrifying, I'm sure.'

'Wait, there's also the sound of the electric grilles on shop windows opening and closing, cars parking in garages and all those bloody dogs. Did you know that the number of dogs has increased by 3 per cent in the last few months?'

'No. Where did you read that?'

'I looked it up because I hate them. I hate the dissipation of affection. Also, they consume a lot.'

'The 3 per cent? Why do you think there's been this surge in dog numbers?'

'It's a constantly increasing number. I don't know a single Roman who doesn't have at least a couple of four-legged friends.'

And so, when it's not surprising us with new invasive sounds, the city makes itself heard through barking, cawing, grunting and roaring, through conversations on the streets and the ringing of bells. Even during periods of quiet, such as curfews and quarantines, with a little training you can still detect the unmistakable Roman trait of layering: all manner of sounds are superimposed on a setting that would be much better off without them.

In Rome what you see hardly ever coincides with what you hear. Over time this discrepancy causes fatigue, sudden attacks of rage, hunger, a tremendous sense of impotence and turns you into a background extra, for ever. Rome is a perception-altering narcotic that leads to disassociation, triggers satiety, has no withdrawal symptoms and, like the very basest of them, knows exactly how to comfort you. 🐟

Rome Does Not Judge

Nicola Lagioia has spent years studying the case of Luca Varani – the victim of a deranged, motiveless killing – delving into Rome's nightlife and trying to dig deeper into the subconscious of a city that seems lost, indecipherable, hard to live in but at the same time buzzing with life.

NICOLA LAGIOIA
Translated by Will Schutt

The main entrance
to Palazzo Farnese.

On 4 March 2016, in an apartment in the Collatino neighbourhood of Rome, 23-year-old Luca Varani was brutalised by Marco Prato and Manuel Foffo, two men in their thirties with no prior record. At the direction of Foffo, who lived in the apartment, officers found Varani's corpse the following night. He was naked, prone on the bed, buried under a duvet, a knife stuck in his chest, and all over his body were countless cuts and bruises made with metal implements (a second knife and a hammer, it was later discovered). The young man's teeth had been smashed in, his throat slit, his abdomen crushed. There was no decisive blow, determined the medical examiners. Luca Varani had bled to death after being tortured for hours. In addition to the penetrating wounds – Luca's father Giuseppe Varani was forced to confirm this himself when he was summoned to the morgue to identify his son – Luca's body was covered with superficial cuts and abrasions. They weren't the cause of death, but they may have been the explanation.

'Those two wanted to have some fun. That's what happened,' concluded an angry and incredulous Mr Varani.

The case inflamed public opinion. National news talked about it, the afternoon and evening talk shows talked about it more. The story dominated the daily papers for months. In Rome especially, from the city centre to the suburbs, it was all anybody discussed. The case was picked apart in forensic detail at home, on the street, in trattorias, in cafés and nightclubs. What gripped people's attention this time was not the mystery of it but the absence of mystery. Inexplicability in the cold light of day is, after all, characteristic of Rome. There are cities in which everybody knows but no one talks and cities in which everybody talks but no one understands a thing. In Rome people sound off day and night, do nothing but imprecate, denounce, blaspheme, name names (first and last), cast hexes, stake claims, lodge threats; and then they throw up their hands and say it was all a joke. That is why it is so hard to get to the bottom of anything. Any possibility of doing so gets drowned out by the noise.

In the murder of Luca Varani there were no bad guys to catch, no fugitives to hunt. Even reconstructing what had happened turned out to be pretty straightforward. That was the problem.

Manuel Foffo confessed immediately to the murder. He told his bewildered father that he and another man named Marco Prato had holed up for three days in the apartment in Collatino. They started taking cocaine, traded increasingly intimate secrets and stoked each other's wildest fantasies until they decided to 'hurt somebody' or – here stories differ – organise a 'fake rape'. They WhatsApped several people they knew peripherally (so as not to put their closest friends in danger) inviting them to come over.

In what amounts to an out-take from

NICOLA LAGIOIA, originally from Bari and now living in Rome, is one of Italy's most critically acclaimed contemporary novelists. He has been the recipient of the Volponi, Straniero and Viareggio awards as well as the Strega Prize and in 2010 was named one of Italy's best writers under forty. He has been a jury member of the Venice Film Festival and is the programme director of the Turin Book Fair. Lagioia is also a contributor to Italy's most prominent culture pages. *Ferocity* (Europa Editions, 2017) was his English-language debut, and his latest book, *La città dei vivi* (Einaudi, 2020), was inspired by the events covered in this article.

a horror film, various peers of Marco and Manuel saw a message flash across their smartphone screens. 'We're having a party. You in?' Whoever took the bait was auditioning for the role of sacrificial victim.

Some of the men who received the message did, in fact, show up at the appointed place. They stopped by briefly and were agog to find, instead of a party, Marco and Manuel, shadows of their former selves, in a two-bedroom flat that with every passing day grew filthier, messier, gloomier, more macabre, a place where 'evil was palpable'. And then, ignoring their hosts' pleas to stay, one after the other they would bolt for the door until – at the end of this delusional casting session – into the apartment walked Luca Varani.

'The minute we saw him we thought, "He's the one." It was like a tacit agreement between us,' Manuel told officers.

But an agreement to do what?

The crime had no motive. When Manuel was interrogated by the prosecutor, he said he didn't even know the victim's name. For hours he had stabbed and bludgeoned a man he knew nothing about. 'Marco Prato was the one who invited him over.'

Marco and Manuel had only recently met. Before then they had seen each other now and again, a handful of times.

'Why did you kill him?' investigators asked.

'Could be a hundred reasons, could be none,' Manuel answered.

'I never thought of actually hurting Luca,' added Marco.

They harboured no ill will towards the victim. There was no animosity or jealousy nor did they have anything material to gain from the crime. In the absence of a rational explanation people wanted to know more about the main players. They soon learned that Manuel Foffo was a struggling law student who butted heads with his domineering fifty-something father who had carved out a career in the restaurant and vehicle-licensing-agency industries. Marco Prato, a PR man with an active following in Rome's gay scene, was raised in an upper-middle-class Catholic household. Foffo was as jittery and irritable as Prato was perennially euphoric and over the top, although he, too, often talked about the emotional voids that had plagued him since adolescence. Both came from comfort. Neither had a steady job. Both – although they denied it – had no clear idea about what the future held for them.

Luca Varani lived outside the GRA, Rome's ring road, in Storta. Born in the former Yugoslavia, he was adopted at a young age by a Roman couple, itinerant stallholders who did the rounds of farmers' markets in the province selling nuts and confectionery off the back of their small white lorry.

Three social classes, three lifestyles, three different parts of Rome. And three different ways of navigating their sexual orientation. Marco Prato was openly gay. Manuel Foffo said he was straight but confessed to having an erotic relationship with Prato about which he felt extremely ashamed. (Prato, in the habit of aggressively pursuing straight men, had seduced Foffo after the two drank and snorted cocaine together.) Despite having had a girlfriend since high school, and despite having published faintly homophobic posts on his Facebook page shortly before his death, Luca Varani had led a secret life, Prato and Foffo later confirmed, a life no one knew about: to supplement the income from his job as a car mechanic he moonlighted as a prostitute. These claims

Sunset on the Via Salaria.

THE PASSENGER   Nicola Lagioia

Night-time on Viale Mazzini, in the Prati neighbourhood.

Also known as Gay Street, Via San Giovanni in Laterano – the street in the Monti neighbourhood running between Piazza San Giovanni in Laterano and the Colosseum – is a meeting point for Rome's LGBTQ+ community and home to numerous gay-friendly businesses. It was officially inaugurated as Gay Street in 2007, shortly after two men kissing were arrested for committing 'obscene acts in a public place', leading to major protests. Between July and September of that same year the area was partially pedestrianised in the evenings from Thursday to Sunday, the idea being to create a place where everyone could feel safe and to build a bridge between locals and the LGBTQ+ community. The area around the Colosseum had, in fact, been a meeting point for the community for many years. In the late 1990s the community would gather not far away at the Events Bar and the Side in Rome's first gay street, Via Pietro Verri; the initiative failed, however, following objections from residents, marginalisation and intimidation from the far-right Forza Nuova. In the early 2000s, with the opening of a new bar called Coming Out, the LGBTQ+ community moved to Via San Giovanni in Laterano, and many other venues in the street became gay-friendly. Sadly, it has been targeted by protests and homophobic attacks, including the fire set at Coming Out in 2006 and a firecracker thrown at people at the entrance to the street in 2009. In August 2020, just a week after its annual street party, hundreds of posters were put up reading 'Gays out, obscene acts in a public place', signed 'The Residents'.

have drawn the indignation of Luca's friends and relatives who have always considered them false. As if that weren't enough, Prato admitted (in another disturbing cinematic farce, this time in the style of Brian De Palma) that during the murder he had been dressed up as a woman, in leggings, high heels and an electric-blue wig, his arms and chest depilated, his fingernails painted red.

The internet piled on: poor kid from the suburbs brutalised by two privileged good-for-nothing daddy's boys. Or: nervous struggling student, son of a restaurant magnate, befriends uninhibited son of a cultural manager – friend of a friend of people in high places – and the two get off on torturing the twenty-year-old adopted child of two stallholders from Storta. Or: straight guy murdered by two gay guys after sticking up for the rights of natural families.

Opinions spread ad nauseum. Disses rained down. Calls for retaliation and other exemplary punishments were aired:

Luca Varani was killed by perverts.

Boil them in acid! Burn them alive and don't think twice about it … they didn't.

If Marco Prato had been a fascist everybody would have blown the story up. But he's an LGBTQ+ activist, a typical radical chic intellectual, a creep born with a silver spoon in his mouth.

Fuckin' queers. #lucavarani

People gave free rein to base instinct, as happens more and more now. Social media platforms are clearly not fruitful terrain if you want to get to the bottom of a story, to dig past the public record, to understand what could have led two young men who appeared to have no history of violence to become the prime suspects in an episode of such awful savagery. Merely attempting to grasp what happened (in cases like this definitive answers can't, I think, be reached) would have required completely immersing yourself in the chaos, collecting data, documents and testimonies and patiently listening to dozens of people (something to which I have dedicated many years and couldn't possibly describe in detail here).

Irrational as the comments no doubt were, it wasn't wrong to think that people, itching for swift justice, desperate to get a word in, to have their say while the wave of emotions ran high, felt – not so mistakenly because of the way the masses tend to converge on an instinct as precisely as their outrage is misdirected – that in a case as cut and dried as it was hard to crack, as void of mystery as it was impenetrable, lay the key to unlocking another riddle, one that seemed impossible to solve, and that riddle was Rome.

Was the Varani case a litmus test for understanding how dark was the night that had fallen on the capital?

That the moment had arrived (for the thousandth time) for every person of good conscience to face up to the disaster that Rome had indisputably been for some time.

At the time of Varani's murder Rome was, in fact, experiencing one of its most disastrous eras in recent memory. The city had been in a state of abandon for years. Filthy, bankrupt, beset by all kinds of delays and breakdowns, plagued by mice, seagulls and other wild animals, gutted by unscrupulous developers, hamstrung by bureaucracy, turned upside down by endemic corruption then freighted with fresh scandals. It was the period of the '*mondo di mezzo*' (literally, 'middle world'; see the sidebar on page 54) operation, a sweeping investigation that brought to trial a dizzying array of city council members, municipal managers, public officials, middlemen, entrepreneurs and common crooks for a spate of crimes that ranged from extortion to usury, from money laundering to manipulating the tendering process. The inquiries spoke of heavy criminal networks infiltrating the institutional and corporate fabric of the city, illegality so rampant not even social cooperatives for immigrants were above suspicion.

The scale of corruption was clear. What was not so clear – opinions on the matter were sharply divided – was whether the defendants could be charged with a mafia-type criminal association (which, in Italian law, incurs even harsher sentences). I recall arguing this point with an elected representative who told me, 'If you think about it, it's hard to say which is worse.' While the absence of an actual crime syndicate – with its rites of affiliation, its rigid hierarchies, its paramilitary arsenal – had allowed everyone to breathe a little easier, it also meant that corruption in Rome had assumed a vague, ill-defined shape. You had to picture a giant gaseous cloud, mingling with the little clean air left to us, which we were all breathing. Where corruption is rampant, people are liable to commit crimes without realising it.

Symbolically punctuating this difficult moment was the absence of a mayor (at the time Rome was governed by a special commissioner) and the presence of two popes, even if one of them was confined to Castel Gandolfo.

Sure, there was still the undeniable beauty of the capital, which could survive any level of plunder, but that just added to

A little corner of Trastevere.

the difficulty of interpreting the historical moment, because beauty and blight were increasingly indistinguishable. On one corner mice and mountains of refuse;

just a block down the road the angels of Bernini and Guidi under a knockout sky.

So violent was the contrast that it transformed into *something else* (a substance both euphoric and brutal, exquisite and crude, like wine tapped by the gods of war) and filled anyone passing through Rome with a sense of constant

In 2012 an article in *L'Espresso* revealed the existence of criminal groups that had carved up the city – the Fasciani, the Senese and the Casamonica clans – in an organisation reporting to Massimo Carminati. Carminati goes back a long way in the Roman underworld, having been a member of the far-right NAR terrorist group and the Banda della Magliana, the Magliana Gang. In December 2014 he was the biggest name among the twenty-eight people arrested in the operation that was later named Mafia Capitale or '*mondo di mezzo*' (literally, 'middle world') after a phrase used by Carminati himself in an intercepted call. The public prosecutors, led by the magistrate Giuseppe Pignatone, alleged that crimes of corruption, extortion, loansharking, money laundering and mafia association had been committed. The clan had infiltrated the city authorities and controlled the allocation of public contracts and funding, in particular those for the operation of migrant reception centres, recycling operations, Roma camps and the organisation of electoral events.

The accused numbered forty-six, including Salvatore Buzzi, Carminati's right-hand man, who had already been sentenced to thirty years for murder in 1983 and ran a consortium of cooperatives that operated Roma camps and reception centres. Alongside him were the chairman of Rome's city council, the managing directors of EUR S.p.A (a public property management and development company) and AMA (the municipal waste-disposal company), the chairman of Ostia's municipal council, members of the 'Ndrangheta and former mayor Gianni Alemanno. Carminati was sentenced to fourteen years and six months at the appeal court; Buzzi to eighteen years and four months; Alemanno to six years, which was upheld on appeal in 2020. The aggravating factor of mafia crimes was dropped for all defendants: this was *merely* a case of corruption, apparently.

liberation, unmitigated excess, a shirking of responsibility that could turn addictive. 'People do whatever the fuck they want in Rome.' That was the leitmotif. (By then Rome was also the place where the most common of commonplaces brushed up against the greatest of truths.)

In Rome foreign couples, who in Central Park or the Tuileries Garden would never dare risk a fine, stripped off their clothes and went skinny-dipping in public fountains, and, if the urge took them, had a quickie in the park. Drunken Feyenoord fans jumped into the Trevi Fountain and, overexcited by all that beauty, smashed bottles against Bernini's Barcaccia. Giant bags of rubbish flew from one palazzo to another on Via Portuense. In Villa Borghese vandals had a go at the statues of poets and, when they failed to behead the busts of Giacomo Leopardi or Vittorio Alfieri, settled for hammering off their noses. Mice feasted in Piazza delle Crociate. Buses spontaneously caught fire. Everybody – with no urinal in sight or confronted by baristas who told non-customers the toilet was out of order – pissed where they wanted. 'This city produces nothing,' complained a friend who owned a clothing store. 'There are no industries to speak of. There's no entrepreneurial culture. The tourism is third rate. Ministers, the Vatican, RAI and the courts – that's Rome. A city that produces nothing but power, power that falls back on more power, that crushes more power, that feeds more power and never makes any progress. No wonder people go insane.'

More than go insane (people in Rome had always been crazy and, when the occasion demanded, devout), the city was *imploding* under the weight of its bygone indolence, even under the weight of its inherent virtues. It was as if that 'warm, quiet jungle where you can comfortably hide' that Marcello Mastroianni describes in *La Dolce Vita* had mutated into a garden overrun with drooping, half-rotten invasive plants. In recent years theatres and bookshops had shuttered at a pace never before seen. The city was invaded by obscene novelty shops exploiting a shoot-and-scoot tourism industry that had no prospect of growth. Dozens of tacky restaurants opened where criminal networks laundered millions of euros. As elsewhere, the financial crisis hit hard. The usual profiteers lined their own pockets. Those who could cashed in on old privileges; for the rest, the economy teetered on the brink of self-annihilation. People who owned property put it on Airbnb or rented out rooms. Cafés with slot machines were packed with the destitute. Businesses flew in and out under the radar of the exchequer. Meanwhile the ranks of the poor swelled.

If things were trending downwards or collapsing, it seemed there was no bottom, no end point, by virtue of a magic spell that was both benign and malignant. Everything was corrupted; nothing was destroyed.

The criminal investigation that was shaking up the city at the start of the 2010s had been given the vaguely Tolkien-esque name 'middle world' thanks to a wiretap investigation conducted by the Special Operations Group of the Carabinieri, the ROS. Caught on tape in a café in the north of Rome was one of the most important people under investigation, Massimo Carminati, along with his old friend Riccardo Brugia. The conversation became, in its way, legendary.

'It's the "middle-world" theory, *compa*', Carminati told Brugia. 'There are the living up above and the dead down below. And we're in the middle. And that means

there's a world … a middle world where everybody meets up … and you might say to yourself, "Fuck, how's it even possible that one day I could, say, be eating dinner with Berlusconi?" But it is possible. In the middle world everybody meets everybody. In the middle world you find people from the world above, because maybe they have an interest in seeing someone from the world below do something nobody else can. And there you have it, it's all mixed up. Understand?'

But that was old news to anyone who knew the city even a little. The middle world had been around for ever; limiting it to the criminal classes was ungenerous. In Rome people had found ways to cross paths since ancient times. The middle world was a mental state, a door to be opened, a secret passage just asking to be taken by anyone who wanted. In 40 CE the seventeen-year-old wife of Emperor Claudius would remove her royal raiment at night and ('covering her dark hair with a blonde wig, gilding her nipples') go out to the slums to sell her body. 'She would step through an old curtain and enter a warm brothel,' continues Juvenal, 'and there, in a cell reserved for her, receive clients under the false name Lycisca. Her procurer would dismiss the other girls and grant her the privilege of being the last to close her cell, which she always did with a heavy heart, her sex still on fire, quivering with desire. Ridden all night by men, yet still unsatisfied, she would return home. Her face bruised and grimy from the smoke of oil-lamps, she would carry the stink of the bordello back to the imperial bed.'

To be able to encounter anyone and everyone. To collapse degrees of separation. In a Rome fraught with inequality and social injustice there were no impermeable castes. At dusk, anyone going out

Entrance to the 'Transatlantic' lobby at Palazzo Montecitorio,
seat of the Italian Chamber of Deputies.

Entrance to the building on Via Egidio Giordani
where Luca Varani was killed.

of their house who had an ounce of adventure in them could, in a matter of hours, wind up wherever and with whomever in the most ordinary of situations or in the most incredible. My future wife, then barely thirty years old, came to Rome from Piacenza to work in radio, alone, not a friend or a farthing to her name, and in just a few weeks found herself having her first real Roman night out, invited to a party in honour of singer-songwriter Franco Califano, where cocaine was served on metal platters and people in the entertainment industry rubbed shoulders with men with political connections, where a porn star was spread out on a pool table in the loving coils of a python (a real python) to welcome everyone. I, too, had come to Rome from the provinces (Bari, Puglia); I, too, had come for work (a small publishing house); and, arriving at Termini railway station with two large suitcases, I, too, had neither friends nor money nor any contacts to speak of. Yet in the space of a few weeks it became impossible for me to be by myself for more than three hours at a time. Not ten days after my arrival I wound up sleeping with the daughter of a well-known surgeon who wanted to be an actress. My first girlfriend in Rome, I thought to myself giddily that morning as she dressed in a room facing Piazza del Popolo, and before the month was out I began to frequent a plush penthouse apartment near Piazza Navona – me, who lived in a basement apartment and struggled to afford two meals a day. I can't even remember how I wound up courting the wife of a big shot at Banca d'Italia who loved to surround herself with bad poets, street artists and new cultural icons (I remember her passion for transsexuals who wrote philosophy but turned belligerent at the dinner table) while the husband of our host, the man who owned that penthouse, was almost never there, stuck working late into the night at Palazzo Koch or entertaining one of his lovers in Ostia or Fregene.

As the screenwriter Ennio Flaiano put it, 'Rome does not judge; she absolves.'

Which is to say that when I arrived twenty years ago I found the city chaotic, vital, generous. True, Rome could also be tremendously cynical, but because of that it was incapable of taking its wickedness too seriously. If you displayed even a whiff of ambition, the city cut you down to size. If you confessed to wanting to work your way to the top – even shatter a glass ceiling or two – people would pat you on the back and mock you. Where did you think you were? This wasn't London or New York. It wasn't Paris or Los Angeles. This city had been around for 2,700 years, contained a rare concentrate of paralysis and rhetorical artifice that had always defined Italian politics, and on top of that it was home to the Vatican, the epicentre of the world's disenchantment with theocracy. Rome had seen everything, and more than once. It was not so innocent as to think that self-affirmation or, worse, glory had any inherent value. In Rome you got to meet people, mingle with other bodies; if you did all right you'd pocket a little money, die and have the west wind scatter the ashes of your memory far and wide. Meat, then worms. Novelty and habit were one and the same in the city. After a week's stay in Rome even the president of the United States became just some other jerk. When I moved here the city was hovering between harmony and disorder, magnificence and complacency, sociability and collapse. But then something happened: at some point the balance tipped, and Rome began to slip faster and faster into darkness.

The city authorities have concluded that they are no longer in control, posting on Facebook a photo of the new ruler of the roost posing in front of the Imperial Fora. The police look on powerless as a pigeon is torn apart. The pope can do nothing when the dove he has just released is attacked and killed in front of the eyes of the incredulous faithful. Arrogant and brazen, the yellow-legged gull is the new boss in Rome. These territorial, omnivorous birds have long coexisted with humans and learned to find food in refuse tips and from bins, but they can also hunt when they need to, as people discovered in Rome during the lockdown of early 2020 when the lack of dumped food on the streets forced the gulls to attack rats and other birds. Human behaviour, says Francesca Manzia, director of the Italian League for the Protection of Birds, has meant that 'we have let them know that Rome is their home'. The gulls interpret the food that we give them as a sign of submission. 'They think, "OK, this is my territory."' Experts are not sure why they made their way up the Tiber from the coast, but it is likely that it was something to do with the Malagrotta landfill site, which was opened in 1974 and became the largest in Europe. Since its closure in 2013 the gulls have moved into the city centre where they find food in abundance, and it is estimated that their population has grown from ten thousand to forty thousand in the space of a few years. Controlling them would require selective culling programmes and, above all, a rethink of waste disposal as well as a ban on feeding them. But as long as we carry on submitting, they will remain in charge.

There was the '*mondo di mezzo*' scandal. There was the economic crisis. There was a political and administrative disaster that caused no end of damage. Grass sprouting between the *sampietrini*. Abandoned gardens. Tourists wandering through smog, swearing, hellish traffic. No other European capital was experiencing anything like it. 'Rome in ruins' (*The New York Times*). 'The city's reputation has hit rock bottom' (*Le Monde*). 'Rome in free fall' (*El País*). 'Not even after the war, when you could find sheep in Piazza del Popolo, has Rome offered up such a spectacle' (*Le Nouvel Observateur*).

But Rome had died and been resuscitated many times over, I thought as I read the headlines, and it would be arrogant to believe that the present downfall was definitive. It was running the risk of being so, however, for my lifetime and the lifetime of the people I loved, plus there was something macabre about this particular collapse: the city below was, figuratively speaking, gobbling up the city above, the dead devouring the living, formlessness gaining traction, straight talk and sarcasm deteriorating into rage. Those who dared to say they wanted to do something good were labelled public enemies. For many people, nurturing hope meant being arrogant enough to pray for the terminally ill to recover, for a giant corpse to rise up from the grave. The city was a sinking ship where the drowning shouted 'Mind your own fucking business!' to those still treading water. Anything left with life in it inspired aggression and the bite of contagion, and that door, I thought – entering for the first time the building where Manuel Foffo lived, the door to the apartment where the murder had taken place – seemed the end point of a long degenerative process, the bottom of the well and at the same time a promise:

everyone will pass through here if they haven't already.

Naturally, no single episode, dramatic as it may be, can encapsulate the trajectory of an entire city, especially one as sprawling and complicated as Rome. But we need symbols, objective correlatives that can give a form to or at least frame, however tentatively, what would otherwise be sheer chaos and evade our comprehension completely.

When the Varani case broke, the media instinctively sought to relate it to other scandals that had left a deep mark on the capital in recent times. At first the object of comparison most frequently brought up was the massacre in Circeo in September 1975, when three scions of affluent Rome kidnapped and tortured two working-class girls and wound up killing one of them. The case caused a sensation, especially because it was read through the lens of class – the class of the butchers and the class of the victims – and took on a political dimension. The murderers were 'fascists' and '*pariolini*' (a name for people from the wealthy neighbourhood of Parioli); the victims were daughters of the people and from a different planet in the minds of their victimisers. A partly dissenting view was posited by Pier Paolo Pasolini in *Corriere della Sera*. After first noting the way that the elite and the suburbanised working class were united in their brutality, he made a lunge that was destined to become famous: 'The reader is faced with individuals like the neo-fascist *pariolini* who committed the heinous massacre in a villa in Circeo and individuals like the working-class *borgatari* in Tor Pignattara who killed a driver by smashing his head on the pavement. Two different classes, the same exact individuals, yet "the models" are the former, those daddy's boys.'

Whether you took Pasolini's theory of anthropological mutation at face value or found it questionable, the massacre in Circeo had nothing to do with the murder of Luca Varani. The violence in the two cases had been triggered in very different ways. Those responsible for the massacre in Circeo were well aware of what they were doing. They had carefully planned their crime. Their desire to do harm was clear, concrete, transparent, resolute, entirely under control. On the other hand, had you told Marco Prato and Manuel Foffo that February that in a week's time they would be locked up with the stain of a crime as horrific as the one they had committed, they would have thought you were talking science fiction. That doesn't make them any less guilty, but Prato and Foffo were two sorcerer's apprentices who failed to keep in check the chain of events that they themselves, in a manner as absurd as it was criminal, had set in motion. They couldn't stop themselves or the downwards spiral into darkness and violence that at a certain point became irreversible. It was as if they had accidentally tripped one another over and tumbled down the stairs into the basement of the human soul. An incubus and succubus who change places from one moment to the next and, in doing so, end up maiming and killing. The murderers in Circeo were blinded by delusions of omnipotence; Foffo and Prato were two monuments to impotence – not to mention resentment, frustration, narcissism, bewilderment and sexual, social and existential confusion. Had their paths not crossed it is likely that neither man would ever have turned to murder, but the meeting of two such criminally shaky human scaffolds proved lethal: one came down on the other, and both came down on poor Luca.

Looking at them I couldn't help but think of the city. There had been periods when Rome had come up against catastrophe, charging into a wall with determination or hurling itself down a black well. Today the city seems more like an enormous, pale, tired, disconsolate body, puffy with cocaine, lacking direction and intelligence, launched slo-mo into a darker and darker pall.

(This drawn-out decline has led to a loosening of restrictions, so that sometimes Rome is also one of the places in the world where you feel most free, liberated not only from the clutches of the state and social conventions but from the squeeze of people, a sensation that, although it produces more disorder, also generates an absurd dependency. I, for one, believe I have been inured to this messy and debilitating – and near total – sense of freedom.)

You can't make out the landing point, can't fathom the bottom of the well, yet sooner or later something will happen. The city is eternally fated to lose its way and then re-emerge. Rome *will* pull through.

But when? And how? Will we live long enough to see it?

I can't answer that question with any certitude. I don't have the strength or the talent. All that comes to mind is an image to interrogate, an everyday image in any other context, yet one which in Rome takes on shades of the Apocalypse. I think of what happens in Rome when there is a violent storm, as if the key to the mystery were hiding under the thunder and lightning and buckets of rain. When there is heavy rainfall in Rome the city becomes chaotic. Manhole covers start to rise, traffic comes to a halt, branches break off and trees fall. From Pigneto to Ponte Milvio the streets become muddy rivers strong enough to sweep away parked scooters. Buses stop running or are diverted. Like a defective string of lights, one by one the metro stations shut down. Confusion reigns in the city. You don't know which end is up. Rusty mobile water pumps come rolling out of the depots only to get stuck in traffic. People shout and complain. Traffic grinds to a halt. *Roma caput mundi*: the universal centre of paralysis.

Rain in London or Paris is proof of how a modern city can, if required, morph into a cruise ship: from inside you can watch the sea raging and calmly sip your tea surrounded by polished brass. Rain in Rome reminds us that modernity is nothing but the blink of an eye in the endless flow of time. As you watch the scene unfold from inside, the city looks as if at any moment it will cave in on itself, and, as it does so, you catch a glimpse of the city that came before it. Were it to keep on raining, odds are the old gods would regain possession of the place.

But that isn't the real message. The real message is that sooner or later all cities will be obliterated by rain. Call it rain. Call it famine. Call it war or an epidemic. Call it time, plain and simple. Everyone knows that the world will end. But knowledge, in humans, is a fragile resource. Rome's inhabitants have the end times in their blood, have absorbed them so fully that they elicit no argument. For Rome's inhabitants the world has already ended, the rain just has the irritating effect of spilling the wine that everyone in the city drinks all the time.

Maybe that explains why Rome is adrift. And yet, permeating a thought that goes beyond thoughts of the end, lies a hazier, contrasting pearl of wisdom. Whatever is afflicting Rome now will lift it up again. 🖒

The Soul of the City

MATTEO NUCCI

Translated by Oonagh Stransky

Evening light over the Tiber from the Ponte Rotto, the Broken Bridge, with the Great Synagogue of Rome in the background.

Rome has a contentious relationship with the river on which it is built and from which it is now separated by its *muraglioni*, the towering and seemingly unscalable walls along the riverbanks. And yet the Tiber is home to a whole world of its own – once bustling with all kinds of activity, now almost vanished – the story of which is largely unknown.

63

Rome on Sunday mornings, like many other Mediterranean cities, sinks into a tangle of semi-deserted streets, overcome by a festive mood that is destined to be short-lived, a mysterious and wordless mood that spreads through churches and pastry shops, one that children think they can hold on to by running about wildly while weary grandparents struggle to keep hold of their hands. Bittersweet mornings that touch the Roman soul, so much so that every time we would like to hold that moment just a little longer in order to understand that character, that Roman character that is simple and complex and that, for simplicity, we define as eternal. But on Sunday 3 May 2009 I drove out of the city under the illusion that I could escape that sense of melancholy that we Romans take such pleasure in mocking with our seemingly arrogant (but actually self-deprecating) sarcasm. However, it was just illusory; it is impossible to escape from Rome. I remember everything that happened that day. It was a turning point for me.

The morning sky was practically bleached by the May sun. Here even the rays of early spring can burn your skin. I was driving an old convertible down Via del Mare, and around the exit for Tor di Valle I turned to my girlfriend and asked her if she was cheating on me. I remember everything perfectly – and not just because the race track was still open. (I had always wanted to visit it and get to know some of the *cavallari*, the horse-racing enthusiasts, gamblers mostly, who used to be as numerous and sharp as the Roman *cavallari* in the cult film *Febbre da cavallo* [*Horse Fever*].) I remember everything because a little later something utterly unpredictable happened, something I didn't fully comprehend at the time but which would change me for ever. We drove along in silence. I took the ramp towards the Grande Raccordo Anulare ring road but immediately turned down a smaller road with a cracked surface that led under the Ponte di Mezzocammino and on to a dirt road that ran downhill towards the river. I was following directions given to me by my brother-in-law, heading for a barge that was anchored on the Tiber to the west of Rome right under the overpass of the huge ring road. The name of the barge was the *Anaconda*. Back then it was home to a kind of trattoria run by eel fishermen who still went out every morning to fish. I parked my car in the spot demarcated by rusty pieces of metal, walked down the path through the tall grass towards the gurgling river and looked around. None of the other guests, family and friends who'd been invited to celebrate my brother-in-law's birthday, were there yet. As I walked down the pier that led to the *Anaconda* I had a strange impression. I stopped. An old man sitting in the shade pointed to the river and whistled. The head of a curious animal, half-seal and half-rat, emerged

MATTEO NUCCI is a Roman author who has studied ancient philosophy and published essays on Empedocles, Socrates and Plato, editing and translating Plato's *Symposium* for Einaudi. His first novel, *Sono comuni le cose degli amici* (Ponte alle Grazie, 2009), was shortlisted for the Strega Prize, as was *È giusto obbedire alla notte* (Ponte alle Grazie, 2017). More recent works include *L'abisso di Eros* (Ponte alle Grazie, 2018) and *Achille e Odisseo: La ferocia e l'inganno* (Einaudi, 2020). His short stories have been anthologised in numerous collections, and his articles, which appear in *Il Venerdì di Repubblica* and *L'Espresso*, are available online on the cultural blog *minima&moralia*.

from the smooth surface. 'A coypu,' the old man said, laughing and throwing the animal a piece of bread as she frolicked and played as if at the circus. I was speechless. I looked at the old man. He looked back at me with a knowing gaze. I listened to the ghostly sound of the traffic on the overpass as it roared past, disappearing into the sky. I looked across the Tiber and tried to make out the opposite bank, but the light was blinding, the shoreline blending with a rickety-looking dock to which a small launch was moored. I listened to the wind as it whistled through the reeds and the metallic clinking of cutlery mixed with voices from the trattoria. I didn't understand at the time, but that was the day I touched the soul of the city where I had been born and which had always eluded me. The soul of Rome is the Tiber.

Until that day in May 2009 I, like all Romans (except on Sundays), had sought out the heart of this unfaithful city in its streets, breathing in the scent of grass mixing with cement in the summer, letting myself be guided by the sound of water flowing constantly from the curved cast-iron spouts of fountains we call *nasoni* (*nasone* means big nose, the name referring to the distinctive shape of their spouts), obsessing over the impossible-to-define colours of the *sampietrini* cobblestones (see the sidebar on page 34). I had looked for Rome on the history-rich streets of the city centre as well as on the dusty, Pasolinian roads of the outskirts, in the noise of traffic and popular songs, in market vendors' cries and the hubbub from tables set for festive occasions, which there always are and always will be. I was certain that if this city that we love so much that we would die for it really had a 'self', that self had to be a perfect image for our five senses when they declare themselves triumphant despite defeat,

since it is bitterness and disenchantment that we experience when we allow ourselves the *dolce vita* that makes Rome a truly immortal city. For me it had to be an image of movement: my mother driving her Fiat Cinquecento under the Arch of Constantine, which you could until the early 1970s. My sister and I open the sunroof, stand on the back seat and holler joyfully to the pine trees on the Palatine Hill as the car makes its bumpy way down the ancient paving stones. My mother, laughing and telling us it's dangerous, makes us sit down. The warm sun of late spring. The kind of beauty we're certain we'll know again – we're sure of it – it'll definitely come back, time and again, for ever and ever. But no, instead we head home. That bitter image, that ephemeral and thus divine happiness, is what every Roman needs to learn how to laugh off, brush aside, comment on with both cynicism and detachment, revealing a good-natured yet emotive side and always concluding with a witty punchline. But that image I carried with me was nothing compared with the river that I plunged into on that Sunday in 2009.

Why had it never happened before? What had stopped me from grasping that sense of transience and of eternity that exists in the river we locals call *il biondo Tevere* (the blond Tiber)? I had watched it flow by countless times: leaning out over the travertine parapets that protect the Tiber's embankments in the shade of the great plane trees, crossing over one of the ancient bridges (my favourite, as a child, was Ponte Milvio, which could also be driven over back then and so was another place where I would stand up on the back seat of the Cinquecento and holler for joy) or from the window of a nearby building, in particular a Renaissance Revival *palazzo* on Lungotevere dei Mellini. I had

A stretch of the Tiber as seen
from Tiber Island.

looked at the river the same way tourists take pictures of it or buy postcards as keepsakes. It was a river full of contradictions: sparkling and opaque, narrow but majestic, life giving and deadly. I had always understood this latter pairing through mythology. Rome, like so many other cities, came into being along a river for practical reasons, but the mythology behind its birth offered much more interesting stories. For example, Romulus and Remus were abandoned in the river; and Tiberinus, child of the sun god Janus and the nymph Giuturna, drowned there, thus becoming a god and giving his name to the body of water. The Tiber was the giver of life precisely because it brings about death; rebirth is only possible after death. This rekindled the memory of that bittersweet Roman tune, both famous and misunderstood, called 'Barcarolo romano'. A man travels upstream, and it's so quiet that he can hear the echo as he sings: '*e quanno canta, l'eco s'arisente*' ('and when he sings the echo is heard'). The song goes on to tell the story of a suicide: a heartbroken

THE PASSENGER   Matteo Nucci

In recent years songwriters and musicians have breathed new life into the popular Roman song and the way the genre captures the cynical, tragic, romantic, disenchanted, ironic and, above all, bitter soul of the city. One of the most famous examples of the style is 'Barcarolo romano', composed by Pio Pizzicaria and Romolo Balzani in 1926. The opening guitar arpeggio is the sound of the flowing river; the voice, heartfelt and direct, modest, lays down the tragic rules of life from which escape seems impossible: 'Quanta pena stasera / c'è sul fiume che fiotta così / Disgraziato chi sogna e chi spera / Tutti ar monno dovemo soffrì.' ('So much pain this evening / on the flowing river / A wretched soul dreams and hopes / Everyone in the world suffers.') A man in a boat rows upstream. More than a year has passed since he found the courage to bring to an end a love story that had been on the wane, but still he feels regret. Where can he find a little peace, he wonders; on the river maybe? The bow of his boat bumps into something. It is a body, swirling in the dangerous eddies of the Tiber. Moonlight pierces the clouds and shines down on a face in the water: it's her, Ninetta. She sought the peace that the boatman couldn't offer her and found it in the river, and now he'll never be happy there again. Some of the greatest figures in popular Italian culture have lent their voices to this exquisitely tragic song, including Claudio Villa, Lando Fiorini and Gigi Proietti; the most heart-breaking rendition, though, is perhaps that of Gabriella Ferri, the queen of Roman song. (MN)

woman throws herself into the river. This, in turn, reminds me how, one rainy winter's morning, I was driving my car across Ponte Garibaldi towards Trastevere when all of a sudden the sky cleared. An old man, deep in thought, leaned dangerously out over the bridge. A guy passing by on a scooter yelled, *'Ao', ma che staffa'? Nun ce penza'! Buttate!'* ('Hey! What're you doing? Don't think about it! Jump!') And then he laughed. This is Rome; this is what being Roman means. A joke about death snuffs out tragedy; disenchantment taunts despair. Back then I thought I understood, but no, I was still far from grasping the essence of this city.

Actually, Tiber Island, the formation that stands in the middle of the river and which towers over the heart of Rome like a stone ship, had already got me thinking several years before. That something mysterious lurks in the depths of that divine rock is apparent to almost everyone. All you have to do to become aware of this subterranean force is to walk across Ponte Fabricio, the bridge that leads on to the island from the famous trattoria Sora Lella. It's only a few metres long and, built in 62 BCE, it's the second oldest bridge after Ponte Milvio, which dates from 109 BCE. The deity that lives within the island is the god of medicine. Aesculapius, from the Greek Asklepios, was the son of Apollo and is the god of life, death and health. His symbol is a serpent that descends into the underworld, a soul that communicates with dreams and dark visions, bringing medical cures back up to the surface. This is the god who is worshipped on Tiber Island. His legacy is preserved by the Fatebenefratelli Hospital, renowned for its obstetrics and even garnering praise in the film *April* by Nanni Moretti. But the power of the island doesn't only come from Aesculapius. It

'You see the swirling grey eddies of water and realise you're inside another world, a world below, a forgotten world, as remote as the city that towers above it and on whose banks it was built.'

also comes from the river's namesake, the god Tiberinus, whose feast day is celebrated on 8 December. The deity's power can be felt most strongly when you descend the steep staircase – usually covered in litter and cigarette butts and stinking of piss and alcohol – that leads to the banks of the Tiber. Walking around the jutting island rock you see the overlapping layers of antiquity: all the signs of *Roma caput mundi* are carved into the travertine, transforming the island into a ship's bow. There are traces of medieval walls and windows from other eras. The stratification of Rome is always a moving sight, especially on this rocky island with the river splashing up and over the walkways that encircle it. And then the river takes over. You see the swirling grey eddies of water and realise you're inside another world, a world below, a forgotten world, as remote as the city that towers above it and on whose banks it was built.

In an unforgettable scene from *Spectre*, James Bond/Daniel Craig and his Aston Martin take part in a thrilling car chase along the banks of the Tiber. Of all the scenes they could have filmed, no Roman would ever dream of seeing two cars speeding along by the water's edge. Who even goes down there? In Rome they're not even called embankments; they're called walls (*muraglioni*). Who abandons the pulsating rhythm of the city above and its *lungotevere* to go down to the edge of the river? These days people do; certain changes in Rome sometimes run counter to the laws of time. But, to be honest, no one ever thought of going down to the murky water's edge before a bike lane was created along its banks and food carts were set up in the dead spaces selling sausages and fries in the hottest months of the year. You want to know what the river's like? Ask the cyclists. They'll tell you how exotic it was at first, but then it all got complicated. Sure, the bike path got them away from the city's streets, which are clogged up with cars and endless roadworks, always pushing them closer to the waters that they so fear. Most of the time they're down there they can't even look around to admire the view. On one side they've got the high wall that slopes down from the road. In front of them are the bridges, which in theory should be interesting to look at from this new vantage point, but instead they have to focus on slaloming between cardboard homes and mattresses and the strange figures that leap out of nowhere. For many cyclists, the fear of contracting leptospirosis from the water combined with the horror, however unreasonable, of unwanted encounters with people who make their homes down there, has transformed the bike path into a frantic race track. Meanwhile people who want to experience what passes for the Estate Romana summer programme today – a poor imitation of that cultural jewel of 1970s communist Rome – and spend time by the river at night, barely even catch a glimpse of the Tiber. So many people descend the steps at Ponte Garibaldi on sultry evenings that the river is nowhere to be seen. It's just one long wall of lights, food stalls, pirate-galleon-themed clubs, lounges with white sofas serving colourful cocktails, hamburger joints on barges that empty their used cooking oil into the river and any number of other attractions that conceal the river in the globalised night, anything to anaesthetise the throbbing loneliness brought on by the summer heat. Incidentally, the presence of all these people even scares away the Ponentino, the famous summer breeze that blows in at night from the sea.

No, people don't go down to the river any more except on rare occasions, and those who do make it to the water's edge rarely grasp the depth of the world that exists down there. The most knowledge-able are the fishermen who can be seen on the banks casting their lines over the murky surface, passing time, waiting for a bite. You look at them and smile. Are the fish that live in these rat-infested waters actually edible? The general consensus is no: people either fish as a hobby or because they're starving. In truth, this is not the case at all. The wonderfully Roman film *Pranzo di ferragosto* (*Mid-August Lunch*) reveals all sorts of things about fish from the Tiber. They're not inedible. But who really cares? The fishermen who come to the river can be counted on one hand, and if they've discovered something about the river and the city they're keeping it under their hats. The people who frequent the rowing clubs at the northern end of the city, whether the oldest and most exclusive (and strictly male) or the more popular clubs, don't have much to say about the relationship between the Tiber and the city of Rome either. When you're rowing all you think about is the water, the thrust of your legs moving in harmony with your arms and upper body; the banks become a confused

blur. Better off heading to Grottarossa and Castel Giubileo and leave the centre behind. Get away, go back to nature. And yet James Bond, true to his character, was right on the money. To know this city you really do need to go down to the river. You need that disconcerting dimension of coming into contact with the river god for the endless mystery to begin to unravel. That's what happened to me at the *Anaconda*. All of a sudden I understood that 150 years ago, when the embankment walls were erected, the city was irrevo-cably severed from its soul.

It all began with the famous flood of 28 December 1870. The waters of the Tiber rose over the seventeen-metre mark at Ripetta a mere three months after the military breach at Porta Pia that completed the unification of Italy. King Victor Emanuel II of Savoy saw the future capital and royal residence as a fragile and infested city. The Ministry of Public Works immediately appointed a commis-sion, and a solution was quickly arrived at: they would adopt Raffaele Canevari's project, which included widening the river at several points, building seventeen-metre-high retaining walls to protect the city and wipe out Tiber Island. Wipe out Tiber Island? Now that plan seems absurd. Luckily, Rome has always known how to bury its worst ideas. It's true that a thousand good initiatives also never see the light of day, but neither do some bad ones. But if we look carefully at this urban-planning decision we unearth a hidden desire for purity that is altogether alien to the reality of Rome and lose sight of the enormity of what actually took place. Tiber Island might have been saved, but what did we lose? Scholars inform us that the most troubling destruction took place at the port of Ripetta, a sublime work of architecture that Pope Clement XI

Above: The *Anaconda*.
Right: A view of Tiber Island (**top**) and (**bottom**)
the Vittorio Emanuele II Bridge with the dome
of St Peter's on the skyline.

The most ancient port in Rome was named after the god of the river: Tiberinus. Boats once docked at Foro Boario, which today houses the *Bocca della Verità*. The temple of Portunus, the god of ports and harbours, which dates back to the Roman Republic, watches over all that has been lost. Even during the Roman Empire, docks on the Tiber such as the Emporium, which was used for loading and unloading goods and marble (*marmo* in Italian, the origin of the street name Via Marmorata), were replaced with bigger ports and warehouses during the reigns of Claudius and Trajan. After the fall of the Roman Empire the city pushed to make the Tiber more navigable and to build larger landing points within the city (which had shrunk in population and grown provincial) so that boats could travel up and down the river. In 1614 Pope Paul V Borghese built a port for timber, the so-called Legnara, where the Academy of Fine Arts now stands. In the 1700s the port of Ripetta, with its architectural masterpiece (a travertine staircase built with materials recycled from the Colosseum, designed by architect Alessandro Specchi and modelled on the Trinità dei Monti) allowed boats of lower tonnage to trade with Tuscany and Umbria, while the much larger port of Ripa Grande could accommodate sea-going ships. In 1827 Pope Leo XII commissioned the Leonine port, a minor dock where the Principe Amedeo Bridge is today. All of this was destroyed with the construction of the *muraglioni*, the embankment walls. A few valuable monuments are visible here and there, but, without the contextual surroundings, they seem like forgotten pieces of history. One example is the Fountain of the Navigator in Piazza del Porto di Ripetta, a monument that hints at the past in name only, drowned as it is by the incessant traffic that chokes everything along the embankment. (MN)

had entrusted to the architect Alessandro Specchi. In 1704 a curved double staircase, an extraordinary example of late-Baroque architecture, led down to the quay directly in front of the Church of San Girolamo dei Croati. A beautiful port disappeared, and it wasn't the only one. The other great Roman port of Ripa Grande, which stood in front of a magnificent building that housed the juvenile prison and orphanage of San Michele, was also destroyed. So were a number of Roman palaces that jutted out over the river, façades that shimmered in the water in a Roman version of Venice. As this cluster of unprecedented beauty came down, a thousand-year-old world collapsed. The new embankment, or what we now call the walls, separated Rome from its river for good.

To understand fully the extent of what happened we need to look at images of the city as it once was. To do this, we would usually turn to the early photographs of James and Domenico Anderson or to the landscapes of Caspar van Wittel (the father of the architect we know as Vanvitelli), who fell in love with the open space that the riverbank in front of Castel Sant'Angelo must have been at the time; its buildings tiptoed into the water under the majestic gaze of the Tordinona Theatre. Personally I have always enjoyed visualising the city through the realistic watercolours of Ettore Roesler Franz, a Roman painter who lived in the second half of the 19th century whose work can be seen at the Museum of Rome in Trastevere, in Piazza Sant'Egidio. It was there that I went not long after my first contact with the Tiber at the *Anaconda*. I realised that his most famous cycle of watercolours, the ones dedicated to 'Vanished Rome', did not capture the alleys and piazzas that disappeared during

> 'I began to spend time at the *Anaconda* and think of it as a soul, a place where the river had not yet been separated from the city. The eel fishermen led me into a lost dimension.'

those decades of great works or even later ones, whether commissioned by the king or Mussolini. His work does not focus on places that were torn apart by reconstruction or on a lost era. His water-colours reveal the mood of the river, the mood of life along a river, a mood that permeates everything and one that I had never before experienced. It was while observing the life of fluvial Rome – a city of water, fishermen, boatmen, merchants and simple passers-by, all animated by the power of the endlessly rolling Tiber – that I truly discovered what we had lost. That massive undertaking of civilisation, the building of those immense walls that we now lean up against in the shade of plane trees that were planted there so we can look down on the river from a distance, blocks us from experiencing the river as the deity it always was, the god who visited me at the *Anaconda*.

And so began my feverish search. Although I still did not completely under-stand the extent of the revelation that had come to me that long-ago Sunday, I did decide two things. The first decision was made when I saw the old man feed the coypu like a circus seal: I would set my next novel there. I had always wanted to tell the story of Rome but had always put it off, blocked by empty rhetoric and bewil-derment. Rome can be deeply baffling. It's so much more than its appearances and clichés, but I seemed to have tapped into the core of the bewilderment. The second thing came to me at day's end, when I fully accepted that yes, my girlfriend had been cheating on me. That was it. Unlike

a woman of flesh and blood, the Rome I loved – while bewildering and unfaithful – betrayed me in order to remain faithful. The city's betrayal was an act of deep faith. What kind of paradox was I dealing with? How would I be able to explain this, much less write about it?

Over the following months and years I followed the river. I began to spend time at the *Anaconda* and think of it as a soul, a place where the river had not yet been separated from the city. The eel fishermen led me into a lost dimension. It wasn't their actual skill or knowledge of each and every bend in the river that convinced me that the heart of Rome hides in those very waters. It was, rather, an atmosphere. Eddying around them and their fast-disappearing art was a milieu of friends and acquaintances, people just passing through, men and women from every corner of the globe. A city on the river always opens up. My deeply provin-cial and papal city, which had always considered its domination of the world to be an established fact but which was actually rather ephemeral, used to be an open city. It used to be open to travellers and visitors of all kinds: foreigners, fugi-tives or those in exile, people who wanted to move forward, people who wanted to get ahead, people who may have known nothing of the city's glorious past. Better off that way, not knowing about the past, because what passes escapes us, and what counts is the present.

While discovering that an all-embracing attitude (and not in an edifying, moral sense but in an obliging and vital way) was alive and well in that open city on the river, in that city of the river, I also discovered a quintessentially Roman attitude to time that I had never been able to grasp with such clarity. The man who taught me everything – without wanting to teach me anything – was named Cesare. With his woollen hat pulled low over his forehead and deep wrinkles around his clear, sly eyes, Cesare fished for eels the way he always had and the way he always would. After submitting people to a tough exam (a cursory glance), he then invites them to sit and eat with him under an awning next to his house, a shack on concrete pillars (in case of flooding) in which he sleeps on a fold-down bed. He cooks on a grill and after the meal offers some herbal liqueur, pure alcohol: swill it around your mouth before swallowing or you'll burn your oesophagus, he says. He lets anyone who wants to know the secrets of fishing climb aboard his boat. He showed me a secret hold on the *Anaconda* where he kept the eels that he collected each morning from his special pots, known as *martavelli*. He did this so he could show off their shiny bodies and tasty meat, so that he could talk about fishing for eels, which in Rome are called *ciriole*.

Everyone knows that *ciriole* are elusive, but they're also smart – and this is not so well known. Man plays on their intelligence in order to catch them: *ciriole* seek light, and the only way to free themselves from the nets is by heading in the opposite direction. Humans, who are smarter than *ciriole*, know that to wriggle free from a trap, sometimes they have to dive *into* the darkness ...

It was around then that I started to understand my revelations, which, in turn, gave rise to the idea of a novel about Rome that I would call *È giusto obbedire alla notte* ('It Is Right to Obey the Night'),

drawing on a line from Homer's *Iliad*. Rome would only reveal itself if it were allowed to sink into the dark, into the bed of the Tiber, the final resting place of all secrets. The protagonist of the novel, a man on the run, isn't looking for Rome, but the story of Rome gets told through him until he finally gives in to the river. It is a story about time, the only great (albeit limited) resource that humans have available to them and which, as mentioned above, has a very special meaning in Rome.

The fact is that here we are all consumed by the past. Our past is grand. Everyone, even the least versed in history, knows it. For Romans, though, our shared past brings up a further question: what use is world domination if everything is destined to come to an end? What is the point of even the most extraordinary of earthly conquests if its end is part of its actualisation? *Sic transit gloria mundi*. What counts – the only thing that counts – is the present. Only the present is eternal, only the present can come back in an identical form to a city that remains true to itself generation after generation.

In Rome only the present counts. Think about it. Watch people.

They enjoy the present and have fun. They laugh at the troubles that consume those who are intent on pursuing that supremely useless activity known as productivity. They stop at a trattoria for lunch when the sun is still high without planning ahead. They drink some wine from the Castelli region. They enjoy the most delicious pasta ever, cacio e pepe, a dish that is simple in appearance only. They shrug, look the other way, wave it off, they're casual, disenchanted. While bitterness may be a supremely Roman trait that belongs to people who have been defeated by history and know that nothing remains, disenchantment is the expression you'll see on the faces of people who sit in the sunshine in winter and the shade in summer, for they know that time is the only true wealth. Time is a savings account that runs out. The only place you can take money is to the *alberi pizzuti*, which is to say, to the cemetery, which is shaded by cypress trees.

Sly, cocky, with a cover-your-backside attitude (cunning to the point of being invincible), a Roman will listen to people insulting his city the way a son hears things said about his mother. Now just hold it right there, he'll say, raising his finger. But when it comes to the sewers of Rome, he smiles and lets rip. This city is a total sewer! You hear lots of people say that, and they're right, because in Rome you can sink right into it. You sink into the eternal present – which can be eternally ephemeral and eternally past but never in vain, dead and gone like all great conquests: planned, executed, earned. You sink into it further: into the trattorias and bars, you play cards, you walk on the *sampietrini*, get carried away by the gurgling *nasoni* fountains. But they're all fake images, people say. They know; they're the ones who have to endure this decaying city with its endless bureaucracy, crumbling public-transport system and neglected suburbs. They're merely images created for tourists. But even those who complain realise that those images are paradigmatic of their own personal katabasis, the Roman everyman's daily descent into hell. Wherever he is and whenever he can, the Roman everyman will try to devour the present, even as the world falls apart or, rather, when the world falls apart because the world is nothing, and it vanishes.

Just downriver from Tiber Island there's a bridge that requires motorists to drive on the left, unlike regular Italian traffic, thus earning it the nickname 'the English bridge', although its real name is the Ponte Palatino. Those who cross it on foot usually walk on the north side to admire the so-called Ponte Rotto, the Broken Bridge, an ancient-Roman-and-16th-century ruin that stands there in the swirling waters of the Tiber like a monument to everything that has been saved from the onslaught of time, floods and demolition for the construction of the embankment walls. If you walk on the south side of the bridge you can see a real jewel: an ancient arch embedded in the riverbank marks the place where the mouth of the Cloaca Massima stood, the oldest Roman urbanisation project (built in the 6th century BCE) and the oldest functioning sewer in the entire world. This truly is eternity. Homeless people and other random travellers camp out on its slopes at night. Perhaps they, more than anyone else, know just what a sewer this city is.

It is a sewer of many things. First, it is a sewer of crime. The newspapers have always characterised Rome as a place of lowlifes, petty criminals and bullies, heirs to the *grevi con la zaccagna* (those bosses who traditionally armed themselves with knives, the weapon of choice in Rome) all the way down to the most pervasive criminal levels, which are now famously defined as worlds and divided into two: the upper and the lower. Paradoxically, the lower-level criminals are cleaner than the upper ones. Countless crimes and disappearances take place in the waters of the Tiber. Some years ago an American student disappeared in the eddies of the river under Ponte Garibaldi, apparently because someone stole his credit card during a night of drunken carousing, although the judge ultimately exonerated

Cesare, eighty-one, has been an eel fisherman on the Tiber
for more than sixty years. 'I can't explain the bond I have
with the Tiber; I can't be away from it, not even for a day.'

Above: Cesare travels on his barge every day, the sole survivor of a bygone world. **Left**: Cesare pulls in one of his nets. There was once a thriving market for eels and a cooperative with dozens of fishermen.

The origins of this troubled tale go back to 2012, when the new American owners of the most popular football team in the city – A.S. Roma – met then-mayor Alemanno to identify a site for a new stadium, which would also stimulate the opening up of the area around it for development. As soon as Tor di Valle was chosen the controversy began: the land on which the famous racecourse was built is a flood plain; the grandstand, by Julio Lafuente, is considered an architectural jewel and worth preserving; access roads to the area are poor; that particular bend in the river is home to an important natural habitat. Cement and construction would mean destroying a world that many people would like to save and, if anything, give back to its citizens, the way Madrid rescued the area around the Manzanares river, which for decades had been buried under the old stadium of Atlético Madrid and the neighbouring highway. But in Rome things move in the opposite direction. In 2012 people dreamed of seeing Totti on the field beneath the nearby Libeskind-designed high-rises. Today, after a series of problems (including legal and political obstacles, architectural compromises, major planning revisions, arrests for bribery, accusations of speculation, political intrigue and three city mayors who were excessively attentive to votes from Roma fans) the project seems definitely to have been abandoned. If, as people have been saying for years, the football club embodies the city in all its madness and glory, it has become increasingly clear that Rome is one thing and Roma is something else, especially since the American management got rid of team legends Totti, De Rossi and Florenzi, stars who were forced to quit, were sidelined or sold abroad in an internationalisation that to many heralded the end of an era. (MN)

the presumed culprit. However, the most interesting kinds of metaphorical sewers are not the ones you read about in the papers but those with an almost metaphysical character: the ones that become matter, that overflow, that spread beyond the margins, beyond the walls and into the soul, an invincible marshy mess that triumphs over oblivion. The perfect and invincible sewer. This is the dimension into which even the staunchest anti-Roman politicians sink, charmed by the clinking of cutlery in trattorias. A place of dreams and quicksand, the very quicksand that drove Woody Allen to nod off while making his worst ever film, *To Rome with Love.* Rome is a muddy, brackish river where only those who seek out darkness are saved.

The river is finally revealing its mysteries. Whosoever chooses to enter into an eternal katabasis will discover that darkness conceals the most precious thing that the city has to offer its offspring: betrayal. That is, as I said, her only act of loyalty. Here, in fact, the real deception is nothing to do with marital misdemeanours; those will come and go like everything of little import. It's another form of treason that I speak of, one that every single life is marked with: death. Every life, all life, human or animal, not just Roman life, carries death within it from its very beginning. But Rome reserves a special kind of unfaithfulness for its offspring. Ever since you were in swaddling clothes the city has tried to show you its splendours. It fills you with the illusion of magnificence and then knocks you down and spits you out, showing you that being born is tantamount to a death sentence. So you sink into the present and let yourself be deceived: it's your only option. This deceit is the heart of Rome. Only by living it completely will you be able to save yourself. This is the real secret of the river. If a person, unlike an eel, can free himself by seeking out darkness instead of light, Rome and the Tiber teach the true Roman to sink into darkness from day one; overcome the deception by living it. It's no coincidence that the best verb for describing what Romans have to do to survive the death of everything around them is a slowly vanishing word, one that derives precisely from the movement of the eel, our beloved *ciriola*: *ciriolare*, to move like an eel, to slip by and through. *Ciriolare, ciriolare*, always *ciriolare*. In other words, find a way to get by, get around it, adapt to whatever comes along, to the present, to whatever the day presents you with or what it takes away from you; slip away, slip away from problems both real and imagined and discover light in the darkness. It is pointless to try to impose laws on the chaos that reigns over us, over sovereign nature, over the unfathomable randomness of destiny, fate, the gods or whatever divinity or essence governs our lives. Time passes. It passes like the water of the river that remains always the same.

It may well be that Heraclitus is behind all these reflections on the 'blond Tiber'. 'We both step and do not step into the same rivers. We are and are not,' the enigmatic philosopher from Ephesus wrote. Everything passes, *panta rei*, they said later to explain his line of thinking, but Heraclitus had already coined other aphorisms of his own. We find 'ever-newer waters' diving into the river, and that is why 'you cannot step into the same river twice'. Heraclitus truly was a genius. Maybe he had within him that ideal and truly immortal Rome that is a state of mind, a meta-historical and meta-geographical paradigm. Because that's exactly how it is here. The river is the same, always the same, despite embankments, walls, diversions, widening projects, channels. The flow is always the same, but the water is always new. Every single unrepeatable moment is already lost within the eternal return of the same. Only that which is ephemeral contains eternity, only what comes and goes, only the present moment. Romans get this and adjust accordingly, constantly circling back, slipping through, swimming to the bottom. The river eliminates everything, it purifies and heals, but first you have to enter into the river, accept the challenge. And the challenge is to live, despite the past.

Rome, in fact, is never-ending. They can shift the course of the Tiber out of the centre, fill its banks with food stalls, stuff it with crime stories and dramatic events or glorify it with the graffiti of foreign artists, such as William Kentridge's magnificent work *Triumphs and Laments*, dedicated to the victories and failures of Rome, but the Tiber will always remain the soul of this city. Those who are willing to take up the challenge and immerse themselves completely in this state of deceit will discover what people have always tried to deny, what's been kept under wraps, hidden from view. And it is this: the name Rome – as Servius, the 4th/5th-century-CE grammarian, noted – actually derives from Rumon, an archaic name for the river that became the name of the city only when the river acquired its name from Tiberinus, the boy who died in the river, becoming, thanks to his death, eternal. 🐟

The author would like to thank the architects Pier Luigi Porzio and Giovanni Battista Porzio for their enormous help on everything concerning Rome and its history.

39 Notes for a Book on Rome

Is it possible to understand Rome? Over the years some seem to have succeeded, but Francesco Piccolo, who moved there from Caserta, is still trying. There are many reasons to love the city, and he lists some here while awaiting the day when he, too, can proclaim that he not only loves but also *understands* Rome.

Francesco Piccolo

Translated by Oonagh Stransky

81

1.   Romans don't understand Rome – or, rather, Romans don't love Rome, maybe because they do understand it, and that's precisely why they don't love it.

2.   Rome could be fun because there are always parties taking place. But people from Rome are always disappointed by the parties: they didn't want to be there, they want to go to a different party, a better one. But when they go to those parties they're disappointed by them, too.

Can you imagine the inner struggle of a community that doesn't have fun at any of its parties, a community that says it's time to leave Rome because it's not the Rome it used to be and yet the following night you bump into the same people at another bar and they're saying the same thing as they said the night before, and six years later they're still saying the same thing, and twelve years later still the same ad infinitum?

3.   'One good thing about Rome is that after the initial impact people leave you alone.' (Ella Fitzgerald)

4.   When I'm out walking early in the morning there's one route I always take that goes down the Colle Oppio and past the Colosseum. I've got the Colosseum on one side, which is gigantic when I'm there next to it, across from me is the Basilica of Maxentius, in front of me is the Arch of Constantine and on the right is the Palatine Hill.

Even if I'm walking briskly it's a long stretch. I look to the left and right as I go and think to myself: I live in Rome.

FRANCESCO PICCOLO is an author, screenwriter and regular contributor to *Corriere della Sera*. He won the Strega Prize in 2014 for *Il desiderio di essere come tutti*. He has written screenplays for Paolo Virzì, Nanni Moretti, Francesca Archibugi, Silvio Soldini, Marco Bellocchio and co-wrote the screenplay for the TV series *My Brilliant Friend* based on the novels of Elena Ferrante. In 2019 director Daniele Luchetti made the film *Ordinary Happiness* based on Piccolo's 2010 book *Momenti di trascurabile felicità* (Einaudi) and the 2015 sequel *Momenti di trascurabile infelicità* (Einaudi).

5.   Once I was on my way back from lunch and I walked by the Piramide metro station and saw a crowd of people looking down into a hole where there were men at work. It was about a metre and a half deep, no more than that, and the workmen's heads were above street level.

Being curious, I went over to see what they were looking at. It was a skeleton, freshly exhumed. The crew had been called out to resolve some kind of electrical problem. Surprised, I asked one of the men about it, and he said, 'We're always finding them, there are loads around here, this was where ...' And then he stopped.

6.   Take someone to Garbatella who's never been there, who has no idea of what kind of area it is, and see how they react.

7.   A long time ago I heard Paola Borboni, the actress, say on the radio, 'I love Rome. And I even understand it.' I liked that, especially the 'I even understand it' bit. One day I'd like to be able to say that. One day I will.

8.   Now that you live in Rome and not back home in the provinces, you start editing your life story.

9.   *Episode One*. After having complained about my bank for years but never actually doing anything about it, one day I make up my mind to switch. The bank employee has me fill out endless forms. When she sees that I live in Piazza Vittorio she looks at me in surprise, with less suspicion and more compassion, and says, 'Wow, that can't be an easy place to live. You have it rough there with all those foreigners and the Chinese. How do you manage?'

Episode Two. I'm at a party (where someone told me about a better party going on somewhere else) talking to this creative type who all but ignores me and just looks around the room as if she were still deciding how to spend the evening. She asks me where I live. I say Piazza Vittorio. She lights up, suddenly realising that there's a person standing next to her. She looks me straight in the eye and says she'd love to live in Piazza Vittorio, she's looking for a place there, it must be an amazing neighbourhood, she thinks, with all that diversity (and I think that, in contrast to the woman at the bank, she actually included the Chinese among the other foreigners, which seems more accurate).

10.   Two women live in Piazza Vittorio. They moved here because of their passion for ethnic diversity and globalisation, two communists who used to throw petrol bombs at the police and chant things like '*Via, via; via la polizia!*' when they were young but who now spend their days calling the police to make complaints. The only time they ever smile is when they see the police arrive to bust those diverse people. The rest of us laugh at them, shocked at their behaviour, but actually we're all better off after the arrests. They saved us from having to call the police ourselves; we can go on being communists, safe behind the doors of our expensive apartments – they did the dirty work for us.

11.   Romans are tired of Rome. They treat it like rubbish, like something of which they've had enough. Actually, they're tired of everything. Romans are tired of their parents, children, lovers, friends, neighbours and colleagues. They're tired of calling and texting, their evening stroll, going to the theatre, seeing the full moon, enjoying a good restaurant or cappuccino, tired of marathons and car sharing. They're tired not only of Christmas lights but of Christmas, too; tired of this year as well as the next. Tired of vacations, overtime, fountains, parent–teacher meetings, report cards. They're utterly and legitimately tired of *sampietrini*, and if someone tries to tell them what makes those cobblestones so unique they might just rip that person's head off. They're tired of things that last, but what's even more incredible is that they're tired of everything new. Almost immediately, they grew tired of the pandemic. They're tired of everyone with no exceptions.

12.   Housing in Rome is very expensive, but, proportionally speaking, in the rank of the most expensive things in Rome, housing comes second. Chestnuts take first place. Until recently people would say that, proportionally speaking, chestnuts cost more than a flat. People don't include the phrase 'proportionally speaking' any more. Chestnuts cost more than a flat. Full stop.

Bear in mind that house prices have gone up recently; imagine how much chestnuts cost.

13.   Isn't it hard to live in Rome? people often ask. Yes, it is hard, but it's also thrilling. Staggering forward through a fug of fatigue with persistence, strength and gratitude is almost like reaching a very high level in a video game, in one of those weird settings that you can't quite make out, and if you stop to think about it you're dead. That's one of the best aspects of gaming: you get to the difficult levels relatively easily, practically on autopilot, but you can't stay there on autopilot. And if you stop to ask yourself 'Am I on autopilot?' you're dead.

14.   Those of us who have to take Line B of the metro to get home feel a little less cool than those who take Line A. Actually, Line B is newer, cleaner, less crowded and has a better colour scheme, just the right shade of blue compared with the red of Line A that always looks orangey under the lights. We'd like to think we're better than them, but somehow it always seems like Line B is a derivative of Line A: you may be familiar with Line B, but you know for sure you've travelled on Line A; the majority of people have only been on the A, but no one has only ever been on the B; everyone knows all the stops on the A, but no one knows those on the B; everyone knows that the reddish-orange line stops at Piazza di Spagna, Piazza del Popolo and Piazza Vittorio, but only a small number of us seem to care that there are blue stops at Monti, Colosseo and Circo Massimo. But the real problem is not the metro, it's Rome. It's how things are in Rome: things that seem older and more run down are somehow better than shiny new things. It's a Roman fixation. Ancient Rome was better than Rome today, and that's the standard they've been applying to everything since, including Lines A and B of the metro.

Metro A and Metro B intersect at Termini railway station. Just to clarify, if you get off the orange line and want to catch the blue line you have to negotiate obstacles and escalators with poorly signposted directions, and somehow you always end up outside only to have to head down below ground again. But if you get off the B at Termini and want to get on the A, it's easy.

For some years now there's even been a Line C in Rome, but no one pays it any mind; I have no idea how many years it'll take for people really to take any notice of it. Those of us who travel on the B treat it with the same condescension and indifference that people who travel on the A have for us. People who travel on the A don't even want to hear about it.

15. Suppose something breaks – your boiler, a chair, a bicycle, an item of clothing, the intercom – anywhere else in the world, anywhere on any continent at all, people who fix those kinds of things would be happy to be called upon to repair them, to ply their trade, make some money. Not in Rome. In Rome such people don't want to be called. They don't want to be paid. They think your broken object can't be fixed. Repairers are fed up with us and our problems. Of course, this makes life difficult, but it also makes us more focused: we're careful not to break things. But when something does break, then begins the philosophical negotiation to be allowed to pay a pile of money to have it fixed, rarely meeting with success.

If you do manage to get someone to come out (by offering a disproportionate amount of cash for the work that needs to be done), they'll take one look at the object and, even before inspecting it, they'll shake their heads. Nope, sorry, can't be fixed. Nothing to be done.

The precise instant that they tell you that nothing can be done, when you realise that you'll have to keep that broken thing for the rest of your life, is a truly compelling and unique moment. Because it only happens in Rome.

This kind of response is so common that Rome is full of objects that can never be fixed, things that will never work again or that will always function poorly. People are resigned to it; they're accustomed to that form of incompleteness.

It's a coming-of-age story, a *Bildungsroman*, one that can be set only in Rome.

16. About Rome James Joyce said that it reminded him of 'a man who lives by exhibiting to travellers his grandmother's corpse'.

17. In October 1972, inspired by Fellini's most recent film, *Roma*, the *Corriere della Sera* newspaper organised a debate between northern-Italian writer Goffredo Parise and Fellini on the eternal antagonistic relationship between Rome and Milan. At the event Fellini mentioned a phrase that he remembered hearing when he first came to Rome, when he lived in a rented room in someone's home near Santa Maria Maggiore. In the evening the landlady's son would say to his mother or his wife, '*Annamo a vede' Roma*' ('Let's go out and watch Rome'). Fellini realised that, for them, indulging in an evening stroll around Rome was like going to a performance, taking in a show, and he was certain that two people in Milan would never be able to say the same thing.

18. I absolutely must write about the kind of people who live in Prati. Prati is like that neighbourhood in East Berlin where officers used to live or where Fidel lived in Cuba. The only difference is that you're allowed in. But once you're in people treat you like a total stranger. If you're someone with something to say, if you have something to offer, they welcome you for a few hours, almost as if you were one of their own. But when evening falls they wordlessly let you know that it's time for you to leave, that they need to be alone now. In a way that is both kind and condescending, and, without actually saying as much, they tell you that you don't belong in their group and you never will.

19.   I don't know if I'll ever understand Rome, but once there was this actor who died young, Victor Cavallo, and he understood it. Towards the end of his life he used to wander around under the porticoes of Piazza Vittorio. He's known for having pointed out that the only thing you shouldn't do in Rome is be a pain in the backside. Even if you killed your mother, people will try to understand you, they'll say, oh, you poor thing. But if you're a pain no one will talk to you.

20.   'If you only knew what Rome is …' (Pier Paolo Pasolini in a letter)

21.   Let's go to lunch. Grab a bite to eat. Go to dinner somewhere. Let's go and see a film and then eat something. We'll have a quick meal and then go to the theatre. We need to catch up; let's have a nice dinner somewhere and a chat; we haven't seen each other in so long. Where should we go? I know a little place, but you need to make a reservation; no, not in the centre – too chaotic; have you ever been to the Chinese in San Martino ai Monti? Indian or Japanese? Which would you prefer? You have to be careful what you order or when you get the bill it can be insane. Pizza, fine. But Roman or Neapolitan? Neapolitan has that thick, soft crust, it's so good but so heavy. Roman pizza is thin and crispy, it's lighter, goes down easy. True, everyone has different tastes …

Those are some of the things you'd hear if you had a pair of giant ears and could listen in to everything being said on the streets of Rome in the evening or before lunch every single day.

Phrases like that or variations on the theme. Phrases that start up and then fade away in the afternoon hours or that are uttered on the phone a few days ahead of time.

Let's meet up for dinner one night. And then all those other phone calls: a reservation for six ... or maybe eight. For twelve or fifteen (but only three show up). I'm calling just to make sure you're open. People leave names. Most people leave their own names. People who want to be clever leave friends' names. People who think they're clever leave fake names. As if restaurateurs would actually come after clients who don't show up or who cancel at the last minute.

Evening comes, and the streets are full of people going in and out of restaurants: Roman, Italian, foreign. Pizzerias, Chinese, Indian, Indonesian, Greek, Argentinian steakhouses, sushi bars, fusion places, wine bars, places where all kinds of (complex) salads are served, a place where they make the best spaghetti alle vongole. I made a reservation at a little place I know to go to after the movie, after the theatre, for later, to get something for a late supper. I've never been there. I always go there, they know me. Should we get a few small plates, or should I order one thing and you order another and then we share? I always get the same thing; the waiter knows what I like. They charge me less – a place nearby, stuffed and fried olives, courgette flowers. One special request: still water only. Just grilled vegetables. A (simple) salad. No dessert, a little fruit, no dressing, no oil, no salt – I'll take care of it. At any given moment tonight or any night someone will be swirling, smelling and tasting their red wine while everyone else at the table awaits the verdict, which is always the same, a nod of the head: good. Finally, the waiter can go ahead and pour the wine for the other guests. The person who always tries to sneak an extra steamed dumpling from a shared dish. Tandoori chicken and rice. Ah, spicy! Some water, quick! A special sauce on the meat. Rare, medium, well done. It was good but it wasn't great; it was better last time, it cost too much for what it was ...

and, finally, the bill please – and those people who scribble in the air with an imaginary pen. It looks stupid, but the waiter always understands. Or the ones who can do the sums in their heads and split a bill umpteen ways, right down to the last penny. Or the people who only have a fifty – or who only have a debit card and have to wait for the cash. To tip or not to tip? And how much? I'll pay this time; you get it next time. Oh, gosh, sorry... well, all right. What? How much? Everything costs twice as much as it used to. We can't eat out any more, says everyone after eating out.

Or else: you lot should come to my place tonight. Come on over to mine. No, really, I want you to. All right, what can we bring? Let's each make something so you don't go crazy. No, really, I'm happy to cook. Then we'll bring wine. (Red or white? I don't know, whatever you like.) We'll bring dessert. We'll bring ice cream. We'll bring bubbly so we can toast. To what should we toast? Watch out for the cork! Ah, it hit you! That means you're going to get married. Oh God, no ...

22.   If you had a pair of giant eyes and a systematic view of things and thought in a slightly more schematic way, you could get lost watching all the bottles of wine (or spirits) travelling in and out of houses every night in the hands of people who promised to bring wine or all the bottles that travel in but aren't consumed that night and then that person is invited to a dinner and says we'll bring a bottle of wine and that person brings one of the bottles they received but didn't drink, and so the bottle of wine (or spirits) starts to migrate from one house to another, night after night, dinner after dinner, sometimes stopping and doing its job, at other times standing in a corner for a different night or dinner until its journey back – because, yes, it can happen – back to the house it originally came from, brought by a person with six degrees of separation (maybe even more than six), back to the person who started circulating it in the first place. And then there are the desserts: *gelato* from Fassi or Sant'Eustachio, the tiramisu from that place on Via Albalonga or a meringue from the shop on Via dei Quattro Venti and so on …

Imagine you have an enormous crystal ball that tells you everything you'll eat in the future, the restaurants you'll go to, the bills you'll split, the things you'll taste off your boyfriend's plate, the fruits you'll peel, the salads you'll nibble on – all the bottles you'll bring to people's houses and hand to hosts, all the people you'll invite over, all the doors you'll open, all the wines they'll hand you, the desserts that have to go in the fridge, the ice cream that has to go in the freezer, the sauce that should be kept out. If you could hear everyone chewing their meals in restaurants and pizzerias and in their homes tonight, saying how delicious everything is … If you could see all the food that awaits you over the course of time in every corner of Rome where it will be consumed, you might feel – at the very least – a tiny bit nauseous, you might decide that tonight all you want is a glass of milk and to go to bed. You'd miss out on the conversations of people in their cars, later, going home from dinners, the sleepy silences interrupted by phrases like, 'Well, they were nice' (if they were nice). Let's invite them over some time. (Pause.) No? Yes, sure. You tired? A bit. OK, fair enough, we're almost home.

23.   The Via Ostiense and Via del Mare, the two contiguous roads that run from the centre of the city to Ostia on the coast, are both good and bad. Life travels along them in and out of Rome, generally at speed, running through the centre of the city like a blade and out the other side.

When the sun begins to set and you're driving down the Via Ostiense on your way home from the centre of town, even if there's traffic, the light coming through your windscreen relaxes you; the light loosens the tensions and neuroses of many a commuter, softening them before they turn on to Via di Acilia to be greeted by those who stayed behind, of which I am one. I hear the sound of the first engine roaring in: it has a special sound,

bringing with it the echo of all the other engines, and suddenly the empty streets are filled with cars and colour and possibilities. I stay at my post until the last one gets home and goes in for dinner, and then the streets are empty again, those streets that lead to the sea when the sea is no longer visible on the horizon.

24.   The day I felt that my nostalgia for the city of Caserta, where I was born, had shifted to Rome was the day I began to feel that Rome was my home. I was returning from the Turin Book Fair with some people on the train via Rome but continuing to Caserta because I had promised to go and visit.

As the train pulled into Rome I looked at the buildings and felt a strange, special affection for them. As the train pulled out, heading to Caserta, I realised that it was nostalgia. For the first time ever I didn't want to leave.

25.   'I walked into a magazine store where I had often browsed in the afternoon. I had never before spoken to the cashier. I picked up a magazine, took it to the counter, and realised I had forgotten my wallet. I set it down and told the cashier I would be right back. "You can give me the money later," he said, waving me on. "I know you."

'I walked out of the store, exhilarated. In these last five years I had made the East Village my home. Home is where your credit is good at the corner store.' (Suketu Mehta, *Maximum City: Bombay Lost and Found*, Vintage Books, 2005 [USA] / Headline, 2005 [UK])

26.   'If you insist and resist, you reach and conquer' – I've seen this fascist slogan written on the side of a building on the Via Casilina ever since I first came to Rome by train and every time since.

Who's to say it hasn't helped me find my way?

27.   I love watching families tour Rome, especially when there's more than one family and hordes of kids.

28.   This morning at the traffic lights a guy in a uniform from the power company started talking to me about traffic and about the city in August.

29.   Bertolucci tells the story of how, in 1959, the director Pietro Germi invited the author Carlo Emilio Gadda to a screening of the film based on his novel *Quer pasticciaccio brutto in via Merulana* (*That Awful Mess on Via Merulana*) at a cinema in San Giovanni on the outskirts of Rome. To Gadda it seemed terribly far away and remote. Terrified of going there, the writer famously said, 'If I don't come back, it means they've killed me.'

30.   'Writing a book about Rome without including a cat is akin to a life choice.' (Giorgio Manganelli on Vincenzo Cerami's 1977 novel *Un borghese piccolo piccolo* [*A Very Normal Man*])

31.   Rewatch all the films that are set in Rome now that you know the city.

32.   Out in the provinces you don't have to be clear or explicit with people because you know you'll see them anyway. Here in Rome, if you want to spend time with someone you have to make plans, you have to want to be with them, and it has to be worth it. This makes clarity essential; you have to show your cards and be true, and that's a good thing, it's something I can get behind.

33.   About anything at all, Romans always say, '*Ce ne stanno 'na marea, a Roma ...*' ('We've got plenty of those in Rome ...')

34.   The upmarket neighbourhood of Parioli gets me down; it reminds me of the way I thought of Rome before I moved here, I'm not sure why; maybe because I used to go there with my mother to visit her relatives, and it reminds me of that abyss.

35.   Then there was the time I was driving along the Prenestina (the road that leads into Rome from the east), and I saw the arrow that brought me back to the present, back in the here and now. I always see it. It's right after the sign for Rome, right before the intersection with Via Togliatti. There's a white arrow and the word 'Auditorium'. I have no idea how to get to the Auditorium from there, not a clue, but if that's the way the city says welcome home it works for me because no other sign does it, not even the one that says 'Centro'.

36.   A long time ago writer Marco Lodoli and I were invited to the Quirino Theatre to talk to a group of students about some schools competition. A few people gave introductory speeches. One of them said, 'Later the professors will talk about it in greater depth ...'

'"In greater depth" is a phrase that Romans should never use,' Lodoli whispered to me.

I've never forgotten that. Over the years I've come to realise how right he was.

37.   You know you're Roman when you start saying things like 'we have to get together' and 'we have to catch up' and then you put it off for months and months and you never actually get together or catch up.

38.   Once the Tiber was dangerously close to overflowing, and I was riding my scooter along the Lungotevere. Traffic had been halted near a bridge. I saw the flashing lights of three or four fire engines, traffic wardens were busy cordoning off an area with tape and the road was dangerously flooded. People were standing around watching. A few pedestrians peered over the parapet to see how high the river was. It had all the elements of a scene from an apocalyptic movie but with a strange twist; it felt almost normal. Right in the middle of the cordoned-off area, and the

reason for the stopped traffic, was a fire fighter squatting by a drain. In his hand he held – and I swear this is true – a twig or small branch, which he was using to try to free the conduit of leaves, urgently thrusting it up and down the same way you'd try to unclog your bathroom sink with a plunger. This man, with his twig, was trying to create a whirlpool that would make the flood-waters of Rome (or at least those in that particular neighbour-hood) disappear down the drain. He tried for a bit, but then I saw him mutter, shake his head, stand up and chuck the stick away in defeat.

Rarely do you witness a scene that captures the spirit of the country where, through no choice of your own, you were born and live. But it happened to me.

39.   'If I go back to Rome, I want to glue myself to it.' (Ennio Flaiano) ➤

Revolutions in the Suburbs

LEONARDO BIANCHI

Translated by Lucy Rand

A basketball court in the Tiburtino III neighbourhood.

Uprisings staged by self-styled 'citizens exasperated' by the presence of migrant reception centres and Roma camps have spread through the outskirts of Rome. Behind these far-from-spontaneous protests is a handful of right-wing groups fanning the flames, passing themselves off as apolitical neighbourhood committees and attempting to give a voice to local people's frustrations – rarely with any success.

KIDNAPPING
[*CASAL BRUCIATO*]

In April 2019 Imer Omerovic, his wife Senada and their twelve children receive the good news: the city of Rome has approved their request for housing. They have been waiting for ten years and now they can finally leave the Roma camp in which they have lived since they arrived in the city. 'The camp is where our community is,' they say in an interview, 'but it's not a home. You can't have a good life there, and the children are embarrassed by it.'

The apartment is in a social-housing complex on Via Sebastiano Satta in Casal Bruciato in the north-east of Rome. The neighbourhood, like many others, is diverse and working class. In the 1970s it saw demonstrations for the right to housing, and, in the decades that followed, its original inhabitants were joined by migrants, both from within Italy and without. These days the tension is palpable, as is the intolerance towards the Roma and other minorities. The signs are visible, even on the walls, where it is not unusual to see posters with the fascist symbol of the Celtic cross and vitriol clearly directed at this 'multicultural' community.

The Omerovic family move into the apartment on 6 May. There is still no electricity, gas or furniture, but it is, nonetheless, the start of a new life. However, on that very first afternoon some of the other residents gather outside the building, backed up by militants from CasaPound, the movement of self-styled 'fascists of the third millennium' that was founded in 2003 with the occupation of a building in the multi-ethnic neighbourhood of Esquilino. In their view, the Omerovic family's apartment should have gone to 'Italians first'. It means nothing to them that the couple's children were born in Italy or that they got the apartment through legitimate means. The atmosphere is certainly not peaceful: insults and threats are hurled at the family, with one resident shouting, 'We'll bomb you.' At a certain point the police arrive in riot gear, but rather than intervening they just observe from the sidelines.'

The following day, 7 May, the neo-fascists show up in the building's courtyard with their flags (which bear the symbol of a turtle with arrows along its back) and erect a gazebo. In that moment the members of the Omerovic family essentially lose their freedom of movement. The family is helped by activists from Nonna Roma, a leftist organisation that fights poverty and inequality, but the atmosphere has become oppressive.

When Senada and their youngest daughter come back to the building after a short outing, all hell breaks loose. A dozen residents and far-right militants attack them, and their police escorts do their best to fight them off. But as they get to the front door the protesters get closer and try to break through the police cordon. One CasaPound supporter shouts, 'You whore, you slut, you're disgusting' and threatens to rape her.

The scene is upsetting, and it's not long before the story finds its way on to the pages of the national papers. Rome's mayor Virginia Raggi goes to the scene

LEONARDO BIANCHI is a journalist and blogger. He is the news editor of *Vice Italia* and has collaborated with, among others, *Valigia Blu* and *Internazionale*. Since 2008 he has run the satirical blog *La privata repubblica*. In 2017 he published a study of populism, *La gente: Viaggio nell'Italia del risentimento* (minimum fax).

Tor Pignattara, the city's quintessential multi-ethnic neighbourhood between the centre and the eastern fringes, has also been touched by protests and stirred up by shocking events. According to a number of locals who signed a petition to the mayor and the minister of the interior in May 2019, the area was wracked by surging criminality – obviously perpetrated by foreigners; they demanded that the army be called in and the 'invaders' driven out. One cause for controversy, in this neighbourhood that is home to Rome's largest Bengali community, has been the presence of a number of mosques, some of which have been closed down more than once by the authorities, sometimes on the bizarre grounds of the 'absence of a permit for public performance' or similar. Tensions with the immigrant community, and with Muslims in particular, exploded in 2014 when Pakistani citizen Muhammad Shahzad Khan was beaten to death by a seventeen-year-old Roman, egged on by his father who was shouting 'Smack him, let him have it', because he had disturbed the peace by reciting suras from the Qur'an. On these same streets in 2019 Saor, a trap musician and graffiti artist originally from Peru, was killed after taking a cocktail of drugs. As a graffiti artist, he was in good company: Torpigna, as it's known, is one big open-air museum of street art as well as a bastion of anti-racist resistance. The local Pisacane primary school is a symbol of integration and acceptance: in 2014 a member of the anti-immigration political party Lega, Mario Borghezio, who had come to give his stock anti-Islamic speech, was chased away by the pupils' mothers. In 2019, after unknown perpetrators set fire to a banner in Arabic promoting the celebration of migrants' rights, the school lost no time in responding to the provocation with a new, inclusive banner reading '*Più semo mejo stamo*', 'The more, the merrier'.

to meet the family, coming under criticism from residents and neo-fascists. Throughout those awful days Imer Omerovic tries to tell his children that the aggression they are experiencing is the result of a big misunderstanding, but at the same time he realises how difficult it would be to explain the true motives behind the violence. Speaking to Annalisa Camilli from the weekly magazine *Internazionale*, he says, 'They know we are being attacked because we are Roma … they get called gypsies.'

What happened at Casal Bruciato, however, was not an isolated incident. On the contrary, it was just the latest in a long line of events. For the second half of the past decade some areas on the outskirts of Rome have been overrun by protests organised by the groups that describe themselves as 'citizens exasperated' by the presence of [migrant] reception centres and Roma camps. When you take a closer look, though, there has been very little spontaneous protest; it has been more of a xenophobic 'strategy of tension' carried out by various political agencies, most of which identify with the far right.

But to understand properly how these areas have become 'powder kegs' ready to explode at any moment, we need to rewind a few years.

PEACETIME IS OVER
[*IMPERIAL FORA, SETTECAMINI, TORRE ANGELA*]

At the end of Via Cavour, where it meets the Imperial Fora, hundreds of protesters are arranged in orderly blocks. It is sweltering at midday on 12 July 2014. The demonstration had departed from Piazza dell'Esquilino a few hours ago, demanding 'definitive action against the illegal occupation that is poisoning life in many areas of the capital'.

Top 7 countries of origin in thousands (2019)

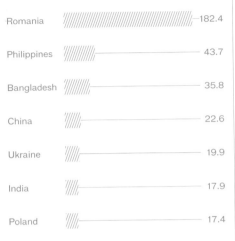

Romania	182.4
Philippines	43.7
Bangladesh	35.8
China	22.6
Ukraine	19.9
India	17.9
Poland	17.4

SOURCE: ISTAT

PERCENTAGE OF FOREIGN RESIDENTS
IN ITALY'S 10 METROPOLITAN CITIES

% and ranking (2019)

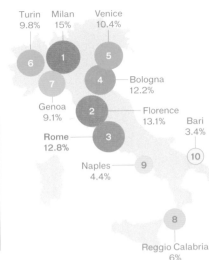

Turin 9.8%
Milan 15%
Venice 10.4%
Bologna 12.2%
Genoa 9.1%
Florence 13.1%
Bari 3.4%
Rome 12.8%
Naples 4.4%
Reggio Calabria 6%

The protest had been organised by CasaPound, and taking part are various neighbourhood committees from places such as Nuova Ponte di Nona, Tor Sapienza and Settecamini. These areas in the east of Rome, near the Grande Raccordo Anulare ring road (GRA; see the sidebar on page 129), are very different from one another: some are new constructions (like Nuova Ponte di Nona) while others, like Tor Sapienza, went up in the 1920s. There is certainly nothing Pasolinian – an overused adjective to describe romantically the suburbs of Rome – about them. Instead they are dropped, fully formed, into a metropolis that has expanded with no urban planning, where unscrupulous contractors are allowed to do as they please and neglect to provide adequate public services to huge swathes of the population, who then, understandably, feel abandoned and try in any way they can to draw attention to their problems.

In Settecamini in April of the same year there had been a protest against the possible opening of a reception centre. 'We live in an area where there is nothing,' one resident said, 'not even the most basic services, and we are already struggling not to fall into ruin.' Lined up right beside them were the 'fascists of the third millennium' and the Euro MP Mario Borghezio from the Lega (the right-wing populist party formed in northern Italy), who has always aligned himself with the far right. His presence in the capital – a city that the Turin-born Lega politician has publicly scorned on several occasions, calling it 'disgusting' and 'as dirty as Calcutta' – is no accident. It is all thanks to CasaPound votes that Borghezio was elected to Brussels. The electoral alliance, rechristened *fascioleghismo* (a portmanteau of fascism and Lega-ism), is also part of a wider strategic plan. The new secretary of the Lega, Matteo Salvini, wants to expand the scope of the traditionally northern party and export it to the centre and south of Italy, but to do so he needs to bolster support with groups that are already well rooted in those territories. In return, an alliance with the Lega gets them plenty of political and media coverage.

This is another reason why Borghezio turns up to the protest in the centre of Rome, closing his address with an impassioned tirade. 'This is the start of true Romans' resistance to decay, to criminality, to invasion,' he shouts into the megaphone. 'Spread the word in every district, because this is the beginning of our active resistance to the invasion and to reception centres. *Forza*, people of Rome, we will fight until we win! Peacetime is over!'

A few days after that march another neighbourhood in the east of Rome (Torre Angela) joins in. On the evening of 28 July 2014 dozens of people come out on to the street to protest about the alleged opening of a 'maxi' reception centre in an abandoned shopping mall. One group decides to block off part of the Via Casilina (one of the Roman consular roads), and, according to the website RomaToday, banners swiftly appear with the acronym AF, Azione Frontale, a small extreme-right movement that is very active in the capital. The prefecture of Rome makes it clear, however, that there never was any plan to open a reception centre there. The official denial silences the voices and halts the protests, but only in Torre Angela, because elsewhere, as Borghezio forewarned, 'peacetime' truly is over.

'BLACK MANHUNT'
[*CORCOLLE, TOR SAPIENZA*]

Corcolle, almost thirty kilometres east of the historic centre, is one of the outermost fringes of the city of Rome. Built illegally at the end of the 1970s, over time it has become a quiet settlement of apartment buildings and houses that looks from above – as town planner Antonella Sotgia puts it – 'like a huge predatory bird unfolding its wings'.

At 7.34 on the evening of Saturday 20 September, according to the first reports, a bus on the 042 route was stormed by 'thirty or so immigrants'. The following day a shower of rocks hits another vehicle, this time on the 508 route, and the driver attests that the missiles were thrown by 'four South Africans' (one wonders how he was able to establish that they were South African, but I'll let that go). As the journalist Riccardo Staglianò reports in the magazine *Il Venerdí di Repubblica*, the double attack 'is dripping with inconsistencies' and – particularly curious for such a serious event – has just one indirect witness.

Despite this, and without a shred of evidence, some of the neighbourhood's residents lay the blame on the fifty-three asylum seekers staying in the recently opened reception centre on Via Novafeltria. On the evening of the 21st a full-on 'black manhunt' begins: two people are pulled off a bus and beaten on the spot; the third victim is a citizen of colour who has lived in Corcolle for twenty years. He's saved from the lynching only because other local residents recognise him.

It is not clear who actually carried out the attacks. According to Lucrezia La Gatta, a journalist from local news outlet Tiburno.tv, at least half of those present in the raid 'were not from here'. One witness tells the magazine *Alla fiera dell'Est* that 'a fringe group of boys in the neighbourhood

Above: Prayers during Ramadan at the mosque on Via Carlo della Rocca, Tor Pignattara.
Below: Some of the Bangladeshi women who work as guides on the tours organised
by the Ecomuseo Casilino that explore Tor Pignattara's historic locations and artistic highlights.

Above: Members of the Bangladeshi community demonstrate against the 'Bangla tours' organised as initiation rites by young Forza Nuova militants. In 2017 over fifty members of their community were injured as a result, some of them seriously.
Below: A Bangladeshi girl at a Hindu celebration in Villa De Santis.

Revolutions in the Suburbs

who profess to be right wing decided to gather on the Polense [the main road that runs through Corcolle] to beat up some black people. They didn't have a clear idea of what they were doing or why, they were just letting off steam.' Over the course of the following week various right-wing political spokespeople went to Corcolle to throw further fuel on to the fire, among whom was Giorgia Melona, the leader of Fratelli d'Italia (Brothers of Italy), and the unstoppable Mario Borghezio accompanied by CasaPound militants. Many residents condemned the aggressions of 21 September, and the neighbourhood committee distanced itself from it.

The script would then practically repeat itself at Tor Sapienza. Founded in 1923 by the anti-fascist railway worker Michele Testa, the neighbourhood is nestled between the Via Prenestina and Via Collatina and – in the words of anthropologist Adriana Goni Mazzitelli on the Comune-info website – plays host to various types of settlement. The first is the original 'workers' neighbourhood' with 'low-rise housing and the appearance of a small city'; the second is home to social-housing blocks that were built in the 1970s and 1980s; the third is made up of Roma camps and reception centres for asylum seekers; and the fourth consists mainly of sit-ins for the right to housing. With an absence of planning and having been abandoned by the institutions, over time the neighbourhood has become a 'suburb of enclaves' made up of 'random and fragmented settlements' that were never designed for 'interacting and growing together to become a community'. And indeed, there is persistent tension between the various fragments. Residents and neighbourhood committees have been complaining for some time of generalised neglect, toxic fires that burn in the Roma camps on Via Salvati and an overall sense of insecurity.

On 10 November 2014 the fuse is lit. The news of the attempted harassment of a girl is the proverbial straw that breaks the camel's back, and the anger finds its outlet in the reception centre on Viale Giorgio Morandi – an oval-shaped arrangement of large public-housing blocks perched on the side of a small hill. In this case, like the last, the asylum seekers had nothing to do with what had happened, but that didn't seem to matter: it *had* to have been them.

The siege begins at 11 p.m. with odes to Benito Mussolini and chants along the lines of 'We'll burn you alive', 'Fucking [n-word]s' and 'Come out again and we'll kill you.' Other residents speaking to journalists on the scene said, 'We can't deal with this any more; gypsies over here, [n-word]s over there.' Another demonstration starts in the evening of the 12th, which quickly turns into something much more violent. Some seventy protesters with faces covered throw rocks and cherry bombs at the reception centre and set fire to bins. The police respond with tear gas. The final tally is grave: police cars are damaged and around fifteen people injured, including police, protesters and one camera operator.

In an attempt to calm things down the Democratic Party (PD) mayor of the day, Ignazio Marino, pays Tor Sapienza a visit. He is greeted by a crowd of protesters and forced to leave with his tail between his legs. Things go better for Borghezio and the CasaPound militants, who are happy to provide yet another photo-op for the television cameras. The press, meanwhile, tries to get to the bottom of whether an extreme-right fringe had any direct involvement. In an interview on the TV show *Piazzapulita* one resident maintains that 'there's someone behind all this. I've seen them [the fascists] with my own eyes. They arrived here and started directing, preparing.' Rome's public prosecutor's office will investigate six residents for various crimes, all committed with the aggravating factor of 'racial discrimination'.

The municipal administrator, in accordance with the prefecture, eventually orders the transfer of minors to other centres to 'discourage the possibility of new incidents'. In the opinion of anthropologist Annamaria Rivera, this 'forced emptying' of the reception centre is an 'institutional concession to violent racist blackmail' as well as setting a 'pretty serious precedent'.

And indeed, at least in terms of media coverage, this model of protest seems to work. 'First the public conversation gets moved on to topics that matter [to the Lega and the extreme right], with an incessant campaign on security, the Roma camps and reception centres,' writes the journalist Valerio Renzi, author of the book *La politica della ruspa* ('Bulldozer Politics'; Edizioni Alegre, 2015). 'Then they harvest the fruits of the problems that grow in these areas, fuelled and exacerbated by the force of the extreme right. Finally, the institutional actors cash in, legitimising from above that which has, on the face of it, blown up from below.'

In December 2014, however, the machine suddenly gets jammed. The judicial operation *'mondo di mezzo'* ('middle world'; see the sidebar on page 54) puts around thirty people in prison and more than a hundred others under investigation (among whom are a good handful of right-wing and centre-left politicians) with a string of accusations that range from mafia-type criminal associations – not recognised in the subsequent judiciary levels – to corruption by way of the hijacking of tenders for Roma camps and reception centres.

According to the investigators, the pillars of this criminal organisation (named Mafia Capitale; see the sidebar on page 147) are Massimo Carminati, a former fascist terrorist, and Salvatore Buzzi, ex-'model detainee' and president of the NGO 29 June Cooperative. In a series of interceptions the latter says that 'drugs trafficking makes us less money' than 'the immigrant crisis', adding 'we've made all this money ... out of the gypsies, the housing crisis and the immigrants'.

Despite the scandal, after a few months of ceasefire the protests pick up again between the spring and summer of 2015. The most significant events take place in Boccea, a residential neighbourhood in the west of the city, after a fatal road accident involving a Roma boy, and then in Casale San Nicola, a wealthy district of northern Rome outside the GRA where CasaPound militants and residents clash with police over the arrival of a group of asylum seekers in an abandoned school assigned as a reception centre.

Around the same period, however, the alliance between the 'fascists of the third millennium' and the Lega ends messily in reciprocal accusations and recriminations. And so a void opens up in the

A petrol station on the Via Casilina in Tor Pignattara.

format of the 'revolution of the suburbs', a void promptly filled by other far-right groups that have been hovering until now in the background.

ROME FOR ROMANS
[TRULLO, TIBURTINO III]

From the windows of the top floor of the Ferrhotel, an establishment owned by the Italian state railway near Tiburtina station, flutters an Italian flag with a banner that reads 'Rome for Romans / Homes for Italians'. Down below dozens of people chant slogans such as 'immigrato manovrato dallo stato' ('immigrant controlled by the state') and denounce the 'ethnic replacement' of the Italian populace.

It is 21 January 2017. A few days ago this building was earmarked to host migrants in transit through the capital. The protest, Maurizio Franco and Maria Panariello report on the website of Vice Italia, is a family photo of Rome's right: there are militants from Fratelli d'Italia, Noi con Salvini (Us with Salvini, the Lega spin-off founded to break into the country's centre and south) and a previously unseen group, Roma ai Romani (Rome for Romans), a splinter organisation that had evolved out of the FAC (Famiglia Azione Casa, or Family Action Home) and which has links to the neo-fascist party Forza Nuova (New Force). The spokesperson remains the same – Giuliano Castellino, a familiar face in the capital's far right and often seen in the legal pages of the newspapers. The group's function is the same, too: to be a 'committee for the right to housing', thus appropriating and perverting the practice and language of leftist movements.

After the occupation of the Ferrhotel, on 24 January Castellino and his comrades move into the working-class neighbourhood of Trullo in the south-west of the city to picket an ATER (Azienda Territoriale per l'Edilizia Residenziale Pubblica, or Public Association for Residential Construction) apartment on Via Montecucco. The objective is to impede the entrance of those who have been legitimately offered the apartment, an Egyptian family, and to keep a young Italian couple in there. The raid is ultimately successful, thanks in part to a rather unusual situation: the Roma ai Romani militants are supported by those of CasaPound.

Commenting on the event, the journalist Guido Caldiron – expert on the far right and author of various essays on the subject – claims that the two groups 'are competing on the same territory' to 'carve out a role for themselves as protagonists' in the housing, economic and social crises of Rome's suburbs. Both take inspiration from the Greek neo-Nazi group Golden Dawn, continues Caldiron, trying to copy its model of 'social volunteering' on an ethnic basis, the infiltration of neighbourhood committees and 'taking to the streets with violence'.

The competition between Forza Nuova and CasaPound is even more visible in another area of Rome, Tiburtino III. Sandwiched between the Via Tiburtina and Via Grotta di Gregna, a short distance from Casal Bruciato, the neighbourhood was once an Italian Communist Party stronghold and the jewel in the crown of the housing policies promoted by the left in the 1970s and 1980s. In recent years the area has entered a phase of sharp decline; there are no cultural centres or spaces in which to gather, speculative construction prevails and drug dealing goes on everywhere. On top of this, three reception centres have been opened in rapid succession – one of which is the Red Cross's humanitarian station on Via del Frantoio, set up in a building seized by the judiciary in the Mafia Capitale investigation.

The far right doesn't miss this opportunity to transform the neighbourhood into one of the main stages in its fight against immigrants. The first group to move in is CasaPound, which organises picket lines to demand the closure of the centres and sets up an 'apolitical' neighbourhood committee (Tiburtino Terzo Millennio, or Tiburtino Third Millennium) to supplant the old one. Roma ai Romani then inserts itself with a more aggressive street presence and a campaign that depicts them as the saviours of an area 'forgotten by the left'.

The combined actions of the neo-fascist groups increase the tension, and it all explodes on 30 August 2017. A rumour goes around the neighbourhood that an immigrant has thrown rocks at a group of children and then kidnapped a woman and is keeping her in the centre. A handful of residents decide to 'get justice' by themselves and attack the Red Cross centre using methods similar to those seen at Tor Sapienza. During the clashes one Eritrean citizen is stabbed in the back with a knife.

For some of the press the episode is the last in a chain of events which confirm that the social meltdown is caused by 'uncontrolled immigration'. After the siege a huge space is given to the complaints of some residents, who tell stories of migrants 'pissing and shitting in the street' and 'doing whatever the hell they want'. The television reporters lay it on thick, being shown around Tiburtino III by neo-fascist exponents masquerading as residents or simply 'indignant citizens'.

But it doesn't take long for this story to start to come unpicked. First of all, the woman who claimed to have been kidnapped had made it all up. Thus the violence is one-directional and aimed solely at the migrants. On 8 September 2017 one resident of the centre is beaten up in the street by four men. Eventually the rest of the neighbourhood rejects the propagandistic manoeuvres of the far right, coming out into the piazza on more than one occasion. In a letter published in the newspaper, some parents explain that 'living near the centre and its guests has never caused any problems, inconvenience or harm to anyone', remembering that 'the many problems of this area are certainly not recent, nor are they to be blamed on the opening of the centre and the arrival of new residents and/or guests'.

So the strategy of the 'revolution of the suburbs of Rome' suffers a heavy setback in Tiburtino III. Once again, however, it manages to establish new fronts elsewhere in the city. And, to be on the safe side, returns to take it out on the target par excellence – a population that has always been at the top of the hierarchy of hate.

'IT'S NOT COOL WITH ME' [*TORRE MAURA*]

For at least thirty years Rome's city administration (across the political spectrum) has treated Roma and Sinti people in this area as if they were, by their very nature, a menace. There has only ever been one solution: sequester them in crumbling camps on the furthest fringes of the city exclusively on the basis of ethnicity and age-old prejudices. This system has allowed many to profit from them, both economically and politically, but has had extremely high social costs and has drawn criticism on many occasions from European authorities. 'The nomad camps,' Luigi Manconi, the ex-senator of the Greens and the PD wrote, 'are at once the cause and the effect of discrimination against the Roma and Sinti people.'

In 2017 the council led by Virginia Raggi triumphantly communicates the approval of a plan to 'go beyond the Roma camps'. The 21 July Association – which works to support the rights of this minority – puts up a tough fight, saying that 'the council is not closing camps, it is opening new ones' in another form, the so-called 'monoethnic centres', attempted previously under the right-wing administration of Gianni Alemanno with disastrous results.

Effectively, the clearing out of one camp is followed by another 'ethnic confinement' in a building, which takes away any real potential for integration. The Roma find themselves in an impossible situation: they can no longer stay in the camp, but they cannot integrate because, coming from a camp, they are seen as a dangerous foreign body. A dangerous foreign body that must be excised, by force if necessary.

This is exactly the dynamic that has been created at Torre Maura, a working-class neighbourhood in eastern Rome close to the GRA. In this area the president of the 21 July Association, Carlo Stasolla, recounts, 'the number of foreign residents is very high and even higher is that of Roma families who have for decades lived peacefully in private homes or in public apartment blocks'.

However, on 2 April 2019 a particularly violent protest takes place. That afternoon a group of seventy Roma people (including thirty-three children and twenty-two women) are moved into an 'assembly centre' on Via dei Codirossoni. One resident asks what is happening and starts putting the word around the whole neighbourhood; the news spreads like wildfire, and soon other people come running. The atmosphere quickly heats up to boiling point: some large bins are tipped over and set alight to serve as barricades and, as always, threats start to fly. 'The only way we can liberate

ELITE FASCISTS

The galaxy of Roman fascism has always been a crowded place, from the terrorists of Italy's Years of Lead to the neo-fascists of CasaPound, football ultras and groups such as Militia and Roma ai Romani and newcomers Azione Frontale (AF). An offshoot of Forza Nuova, AF is active in the east of Rome, where it has distinguished itself with boorish publicity stunts such as its shameful posters inviting people to boycott foreign-owned shops. The movement has also opened a so-called 'cultural outpost' called Pendragon. The invitation to the launch event was signed 'Warrior poets, heroic condottieri!' Their leader, Ernesto Moroni, has yet to demonstrate his poetic talents, but in the meantime, after a plea bargain, he received a ten-month sentence for sending three pigs' heads to the Jewish community. But in 2019 the world of Roman fascism saw the appearance of a mysterious new name in an incredible video posted on social media in a stunt worthy of a Central American drug lord. It was posted by Fabio Gaudenzi, aka Rommel, who appeared in a balaclava holding a pistol. 'The police are coming to arrest me, and I will surrender as a political prisoner,' he proclaimed. 'Since 1992 I have belonged to an elite far-right group, the Fascists of Roma Nord led by Massimo Carminati.' He went on to express his desire 'to be tried for membership of an armed gang' and was at pains not to be seen as a mafioso. 'Carminati hates the Mafia, he hates drugs, and so do I.' Next came the promises – to reveal who ordered the murder of Fabrizio Piscitelli, leader of the Lazio ultras and drug trafficker, who was killed in 2019 – and the threats as he read out a list of people 'who thought it was a good idea to treat us like shit'.

ourselves is to torch the building,' one man shouts.

Before long the militants of CasaPound, Forza Nuova and Azione Frontale swoop in, backing up the protest and streaming it live on Facebook. The siege gives rise to a chilling incident: the evening meal meant for the Roma residents is thrown to the floor and stamped on to a chant of 'You will starve to death.' In the evening a car rented by the cooperative running the centre is set ablaze. During the night the council concedes and – as happened in Tor Sapienza – announces that the centre will be emptied and the guests transferred to other sites.

For some residents and the neo-fascist militants, however, this announcement is not enough: they want the Roma gone *immediately*. The following morning another demonstration is called on Via dei Codirossoni, with leftist activists and residents of Torre Maura going there to express their support for the people barricaded inside the centre. That's when words fly between CasaPound supporters and a local teenager called Simone. After patiently listening to them, the fifteen-year-old accuses CasaPound of 'using people's anger to scrape together votes' adding that 'this thing you do of always attacking the minorities is not cool with me'. The neo-fascists ask him what political faction he belongs to, but Simone explains that he doesn't and proudly claims his territorial belonging: 'I'm from Torre Maura, which is a diverse place.'

The video goes viral and shatters the rhetoric that the far right has been artfully constructing since 2014. The mere existence of young people like Simone means that not all the residents are taking out their anger on whoever is worse off than them, not all are willing to be weaponised by external forces and certainly not all

want to be seen as racist. 'It is not true that all is lost,' the Nonna Roma activist Alberto Campailla writes in the magazine *Jacobin*. 'There is a network of people and associations who move in these neighbourhoods and work to support the least advantaged people, even if the climate has been deeply changed in the city and the country.'

This is seen clearly at Casal Bruciato. After the rape threat directed at Senada Omerovic, anti-fascist movements and associations organise a well-attended protest in the streets of the neighbourhood, forcing CasaPound to leave the courtyard of the building and remove their gazebo. Eventually the family was able to stay in the home they were lawfully assigned. As Campailla notes, moreover, the vast majority of the neighbourhood's residents did not take to the streets to hunt down the Omerovic family. After all, on closer inspection it was only a tiny minority who took part in the 'black manhunt' in Corcolle. The same goes for the stones thrown at the reception centre in Tor Sapienza; and in other areas the solidarity of the residents prevailed over all these forms of intolerance.

The crucial point, maintain researchers Caterina Froio, Pietro Castelli Gattinara and Tommaso Vitale in an article published in the magazine *il Mulino*, is that the far right 'does not speak for or represent the social malaise. It creates it through a strategy that is focused entirely on public communications' and by creating a media spectacle.

In other words, it is not the suburbs of Rome that are in need of the far right, it is the far right that is in need of the suburbs of Rome, aggravating the conflict and offering false solutions to real problems that will continue unresolved even after the last TV camera has stopped rolling. ✒

Maps of Inequality

#Mapparoma is a project, initiated in February 2016, that aims to combine scientific rigour with accessibility, presenting easily digestible data about the neighbourhoods of Rome and representing them in map form to highlight the profound socio-economic differences that exist across the city. The idea is to provide a means of understanding how the city is changing for its inhabitants and for all who love Rome and want to get to know it better as well as for officials who need to develop and shape policies, researchers involved in the detailed study of urban dynamics and journalists wanting to add greater depth to their stories. Data and maps display the city's urban, demographic, social, economic and political characteristics in detail and enable us to compare Rome with Milan, Naples and Turin in various ways. In October 2019 the first twenty-six maps posted on the www.mapparoma.info blog were published in a revised version and included in the book, published by Donzelli that same year, *Le mappe della disuguaglianza: Una geografia sociale metropolitana* ('Maps of Inequality: A Metropolitan Social Geography'). The co-founders of the project and writers of the blog are **Keti Lelo**, a researcher in the department of corporate economics at Roma Tre University, **Salvatore Monni**, associate professor in the department of economics at Roma Tre, and **Federico Tomassi**, a director at the Italian Revenue Agency.

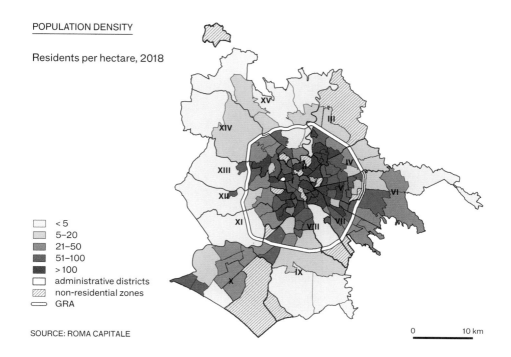

POPULATION DENSITY

Residents per hectare, 2018

- [ ] < 5
- [ ] 5–20
- [ ] 21–50
- [ ] 51–100
- [ ] > 100
- [ ] administrative districts
- [ ] non-residential zones
- [ ] GRA

SOURCE: ROMA CAPITALE

0   10 km

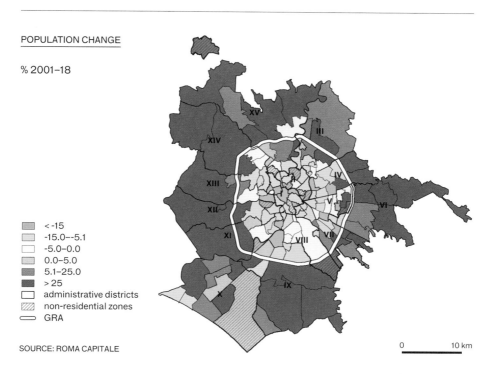

POPULATION CHANGE

% 2001–18

- [ ] < -15
- [ ] -15.0–-5.1
- [ ] -5.0–0.0
- [ ] 0.0–5.0
- [ ] 5.1–25.0
- [ ] > 25
- [ ] administrative districts
- [ ] non-residential zones
- [ ] GRA

SOURCE: ROMA CAPITALE

0   10 km

Maps of Inequality

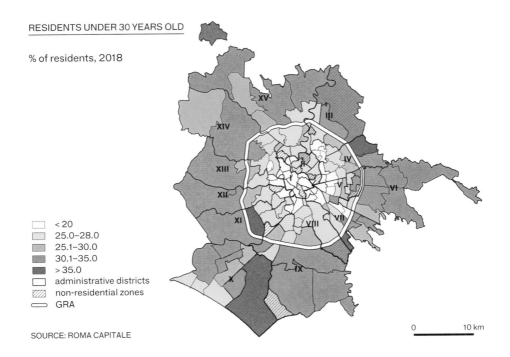

RESIDENTS UNDER 30 YEARS OLD

% of residents, 2018

- < 20
- 25.0–28.0
- 25.1–30.0
- 30.1–35.0
- > 35.0
- administrative districts
- non-residential zones
- GRA

SOURCE: ROMA CAPITALE

0   10 km

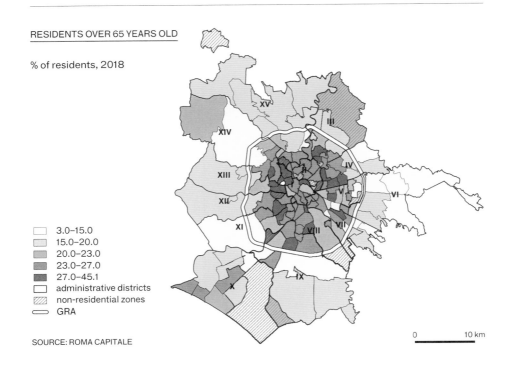

RESIDENTS OVER 65 YEARS OLD

% of residents, 2018

- 3.0–15.0
- 15.0–20.0
- 20.0–23.0
- 23.0–27.0
- 27.0–45.1
- administrative districts
- non-residential zones
- GRA

SOURCE: ROMA CAPITALE

0   10 km

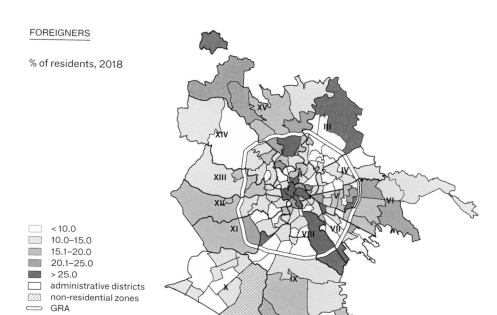

FOREIGNERS

% of residents, 2018

- ☐ < 10.0
- ☐ 10.0–15.0
- ☐ 15.1–20.0
- ☐ 20.1–25.0
- ☐ > 25.0
- ☐ administrative districts
- ▨ non-residential zones
- ⬭ GRA

SOURCE: ROMA CAPITALE

0   10 km

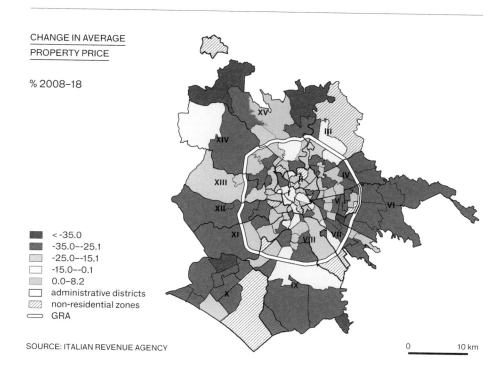

CHANGE IN AVERAGE
PROPERTY PRICE

% 2008–18

- ☐ < -35.0
- ☐ -35.0–-25.1
- ☐ -25.0–-15.1
- ☐ -15.0–-0.1
- ☐ 0.0–8.2
- ☐ administrative districts
- ▨ non-residential zones
- ⬭ GRA

SOURCE: ITALIAN REVENUE AGENCY

0   10 km

Maps of Inequality

FAMILIES IN DANGER OF FALLING INTO ECONOMIC HARDSHIP

% 2011

ROME

MILAN

TURIN

NAPLES

- ☐ 0.0–1.5
- ☐ 1.5–2.5
- ☐ 2.5–3.0
- ☐ 3.0–5.0
- ☐ 5.0–10.0
- ■ >10

SOURCE: ISTAT

0   10   20 km

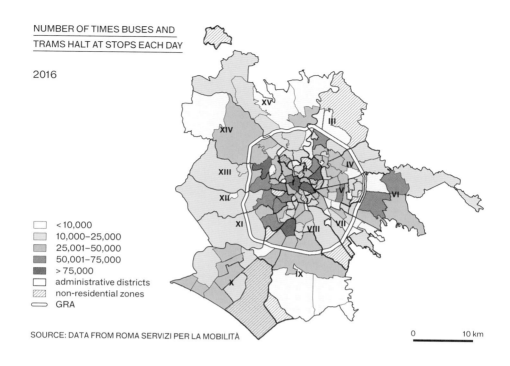

NUMBER OF TIMES BUSES AND
TRAMS HALT AT STOPS EACH DAY

2016

☐ < 10,000
▨ 10,000–25,000
▨ 25,001–50,000
▨ 50,001–75,000
■ > 75,000
☐ administrative districts
▨ non-residential zones
⬭ GRA

SOURCE: DATA FROM ROMA SERVIZI PER LA MOBILITÀ

0   10 km

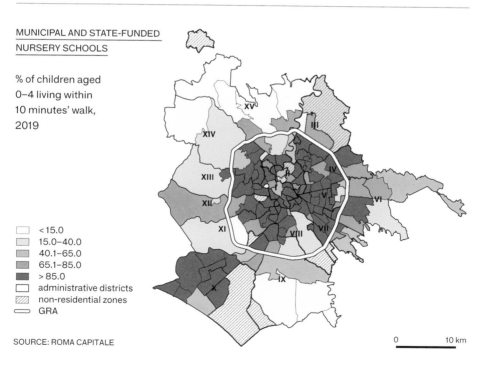

MUNICIPAL AND STATE-FUNDED
NURSERY SCHOOLS

% of children aged
0–4 living within
10 minutes' walk,
2019

☐ < 15.0
▨ 15.0–40.0
▨ 40.1–65.0
▨ 65.1–85.0
■ > 85.0
☐ administrative districts
▨ non-residential zones
⬭ GRA

SOURCE: ROMA CAPITALE

0   10 km

A look-out observes Rome from his vantage point
high up in the Corviale.

The Echo of the Fall

Rome does everything to excess, from its size to its problems and even its monstrosities. Christian Raimo investigates this phenomenon by focusing on a slice of the city, an area that extends from the old working-class districts of Fidene and Settebagni to the Marcigliana Nature Reserve, taking in along the way property speculation, what was once Europe's most polluting rubbish dump and its largest shopping centre.

CHRISTIAN RAIMO
Translated by Alan Thawley

125

I have never spent more than thirty days in a row away from Rome – perhaps *twenty, eighteen* – so every time I read a book, an article or a guide to my city, I'm inclined to dismiss it. You don't know Rome like I do, I think, you haven't *endured* it like I have.

For a few years now, even away from the tourist trail of the historic centre, Rome's bookshops have had dedicated sections for books about the city; first it was just a shelf, now it's a whole department, and my battle against the army of portraits of the city is growing ever more exhausting as a result. Thousand-page monographs, lavishly illustrated books of urban architecture but, above all, a slew of secret, unusual, unique guides to the new, undiscovered, unexpected and off-beat side of Rome. A new kind of tourism that does things differently, going beyond the usual itineraries, visiting underground Rome and its catacombs, the modern city rather than the ancient, the rational city rather than the Baroque. They ask us to trust them and not the others, unveiling their mystery boxes and suggesting they contain a piece of trickery or psychomagic to make us immortal in the Eternal City – at least for a weekend.

In the era of global tourism Rome sells itself in the way that suits it best: by painting itself as the exception. Not *prima inter pares*, first among equals, but *caput mundi*, capital of the world, known to the Romans simply as 'the City', *civitas terrestris*, the earthly city, a reflection of *civitas dei*, the city of God.

Like disgraced members of the nobility, even in decline it knows it represents a pinnacle: has there been a more ruinous fall of an empire? Can't we still hear the echo of the collapse in every two-thousand-year-old relic? In Rome *The Great Beauty* lies not in the past but in defeat: not just the power to make a party fail, as the protagonist of Sorrentino's film says, but the joy of witnessing the disaster, contemplating the catastrophe, the bodies left on the ground. Even in degradation Rome proclaims herself a heroine: the overflowing bins, the metro stations closed for months at a time and the pervasive, permanent traffic do not convey the idea. Accustomed to the rhetoric of catastrophe, the horoscopes of the Apocalypse, the Eternal City does not apologise; it is merely aware it can survive any type of suicide.

The magnificence of Rome is unassailable because it is even apparent in the monsters it has created. The so-called 'Big Snake' of the Corviale housing project is the most obvious example. Nowadays tourists might extend their guided tours and come out as far as the Corviale from St Peter's to drive past the monster in their coaches: a kilometre-long housing complex, the Big Snake, the Space Shuttle, the Transatlantic Liner, the Colossus. And the fascination of this giant building bedded down on the hills of Portuense is undeniable, a combination of the feeling of alienation that results from not being able to take it all in at once, what Kant would call the 'sublime appeal' of the endless

CHRISTIAN RAIMO is a Roman teacher, journalist and writer who is also a committed front-line activist in Rome's Municipio III as a councillor for culture. He has published three collections of short stories as well as essays and novels. His latest book is *Contro l'identità italiana* (Einaudi, 2019), and he is the author of a book about teenage fascists, *Ho 16 anni e sono fascista: Indagine sui ragazzi e l'estrema destra* (Piemme, 2018). A contributor to *Internazionale* and other newspapers, he is also one of the founders of the literary blog *minima&moralia*.

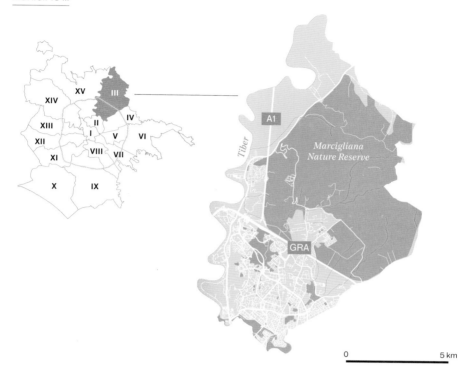

0   5 km

mass of concrete, and even the very contemporary seduction of the aesthetics of failure. This is the Corviale: a place symbolising (in spite of itself) a dialectic of Enlightenment that turned it into a Piranesian nightmare from the outset. It was designed in the 1970s by Mario Fiorentino, who intended it – following the example of Le Corbusier's Unité d'Habitation in Marseille – to be an embodiment of the utopia of collective social housing, but this idealistic spirit proved overly optimistic as the development had already turned into anything but a utopia before the apartments were even delivered to the tenants. For years the ideal town that should have been (a thousand families living in multi-storey blocks around a public square all located on one floor – the fourth – with shops, studios and theatres) instead came to epitomise the opposite: decline, marginalisation, poverty and alienation. Like Le Vele di Scampia on the outskirts of Naples, Palermo's Zen neighbourhood or Quarto Oggiaro in Milan, these are the troubled legacies of local authorities guilty of neglect, incompetence or making the mistake of surrendering to the developers. The extent of people's hostility gave rise to urban legends such as the claim that the giant building was robbing Rome of air, its massive bulk blocking the refreshing Ponentino wind, or the suggestion that Mario Fiorentino died of a heart attack on seeing his Frankenstein's monster completed. A kilometre of homes with no services, broken lifts, occupied apartments with no utilities, it is still there; the concrete mythology of every failure of urban planning. Decades of rehabilitation plans, some of them even very well thought out, have not touched this manifestation of the inconceivable.

Another example is Malagrotta, which was Europe's largest rubbish tip, a hole the size of an entire vast neighbourhood. Between 1974 and 2013 it swallowed up Rome's refuse: 240 hectares, up to five thousand tonnes a day. A mountain range of rubbish owned by the Mephisto-phelian figure of Manlio Cerroni, who still manages a significant portion of Rome's waste processing. Born in 1926 in Pisoniano in the province of Rome, in his mid-nineties he remains unstoppable. A few years ago he started his own blog, in which he communicates every day with letters to the newspapers, veiled threats and gibes worthy of Gabriele D'Annunzio. The biography on his blog states:

At work they call me 'the Lawyer', the press in recent years has dubbed me 'the Supremo' and my enemies know me as 'the Monopolist', but I am merely the single person who made it possible to progress from the old-fashioned method of collecting rubbish with a cart that we used in 1944 to an innovative, industrial system. While awaiting the decision on his request for honorary citizenship of the city, he maintains: They call me the Monopolist, but my monopoly benefits the citizens who make use of it, who have received a service at Italy's lowest prices, night and day, for over thirty years, generating significant savings for all the people of Rome.

This low-cost service was what politicians, even within the best-run administrations, traded against public health. The area around Malagrotta was and remains one of the most polluted in Italy, and the landfill and its ghost are like a foetid picture of Dorian Gray that for half a century has permitted the inhabi-tants of the rest of Rome to live as if they were not creating a pollution catastrophe as eternal as the walls and churches of the city.

Today anyone describing a city tries to sum up its soul in a symbol, a relic preserved in a drop of amber – in *Maximum City: Bombay Lost and Found* (Vintage Books, 2005 [USA] / Headline, 2005 [UK]) Suketu Mehta describes Mumbai as a golden songbird, writing that 'Bombay is all about transaction – *dhandha*' – or attempts to find its lost soul – in *The Last London* (Oneworld, 2017) Iain Sinclair writes that London is 'everywhere', 'one city is another city … more a part of other expanded urban conurbations than of England … London was everywhere, but it had lost its soul.' But since the point in the new millennium when the urban population overtook the non-urban popu-lation for the first time in human history, we city-dwellers have oscillated between an unconscious concern that our sense of belonging might evaporate or melt away like make-up on contact with the burning, poisonous air, as we find ourselves part of a single agglomeration of buildings and blocks, and the equally uncon-scious desire to deurbanise ourselves, to rediscover a wild, untameable, renegade spirit. Or, out of fear, we fixate on a city's defining features like mental life-savers. And in Rome, a city whose only self-image derives from the past, this is even more the case. My city knows it must match up to the images of those who lay claim to it, so it accepts it must resemble itself and be stubbornly extraordinary, regardless of whether this distinction is actually a stigma or whether by 'eternal' we essentially mean it is irredeemable.

Opposing this concept means transforming yourself from a *genius loci* into a citizen of nowhere or losing your identity. And this is the only form of love that you can give to an oedipal city like Rome: to wean yourself even if the great urban mother does not permit it. The final scene of Pasolini's *Accattone* ('Beggar') reveals the profound dream of those who live here, which is to die here. With the police on his tail, Vittorio Cataldi, aka the eponymous 'Accattone', escapes on a motorbike but crashes on a bend beside the Tiber. Sprawled on the street, half in sunlight and struggling to breathe, his last words come easily: 'Ah, now I'm all right.' Because Rome is a city in which it becomes more and more difficult to live, but you are permitted to survive and get by from day to day. Consequently, wanting to change it or even describe it differently is a clear act of *lèse-majesté*.

The betrayal in question, my betrayal, my resistance, my unsolicited demonstration of loyalty, is to think about Rome as a normal city, an ordinary, anonymous city, to extricate it from the spell cast by the trappings of its past, free it from the aura, remove the enchantment and attempt to halt the process by which history is immediately oxidised into legend.

The first simple way to do this is to look at the city on Google Maps and reduce it to numbers. You immediately realise that the magic circle that seems to surround it, the ring road, the GRA, is a magic trick that doesn't work. Valerio Mattioli explains this well in his book *Remoria: La città invertita* (minimum fax, 2019), which examines an alternative reality in which Rome was founded by Remus rather than of Romulus:

THE HOLY GRA

There is a back-to-front logic to the story of the GRA, Rome's orbital motorway. First came the acronym and only later was the full appellation – Grande Raccordo Anulare (Great Orbital Interchange) – created to fit the acronym, which was, in fact, the surname of the first president of ANAS (the Italian road-building agency) and the engineer who initiated the construction in 1946, Eugenio Gra. Similarly, the massive construction project preceded the urbanisation of the city's outskirts rather than accompanying it and was at the time heavily criticised, not only for its distance from the centre and its exorbitant cost but because, in the eyes of the public, it did not seem to be a priority in a country still scarred by the war. At sixty-nine kilometres in length it was and remains Italy's longest urban motorway, but over time the city has outgrown it. The ring road is too congested – one of the busiest and most accident-blighted stretches of road in the country – and for twenty years or so rumours have been circulating that a new orbital road could be built further out, possibly to be named the New Orbital Infrastructure. Meanwhile the GRA has become more than just a part of the road network for the drivers of Lazio, it has entered Italian mythology, first and foremost thanks to comedian Corrado Guzzanti, whose parody song about the road became a cult anthem in 2001, the year A.S. Roma won the Italian Serie A football league for only the third time in its history, and Guzzanti sang it at the Circus Maximus in front of a million fans. But as well as popular culture, it has also been celebrated in high culture, elevated to mystical status in *Sacro Gra* ('The Holy GRA'), a research project investigating the city's outskirts that led to a book, an exhibition and, most notably, Gianfranco Rosi's documentary, which won a Golden Lion at the Venice Film Festival in 2013.

Above: Carlo and Marco keep two horses in a makeshift shelter in the Corviale.
Opposite: Carlo (top) has always lived in Cinquina but regrets the fact that over time neighbourhoods like his have been losing their sense of community. Playing in the piazza behind the Corviale (centre), while former boxer Cesare, eighty, (bottom) is one of the supporters of the Corviale boxing gym.

THE PASSENGER   Christian Raimo

The GRA isn't a ring around anything. The distance that separates it from the city centre averages eleven kilometres. But outside the GRA the city continues, expanding along both axes, overflowing through inertia like saliva driven by blind apathy. Once you have passed the GRA heading east, the urban stretch of the Via Casilina carries on for another ten kilometres.

But the trick doesn't even work within the ring road. Rome is a half-city, frayed and anarchic. The built-up areas alternate with vast expanses of disorganised, anti-modern green space, open ground, countryside and even woodland: to the east 648 hectares of the Valle dell'Aniene, 3,400 hectares of the Appia Antica Regional Park to the south, 740 hectares of the Insugherata Nature Reserve to the north and then, biggest of them all, the Marcigliana Nature Reserve to the north-east, covering 4,729 hectares.

On the official site you read that the Marcigliana Reserve is in a state of total neglect, but what does this mean exactly? The Marcigliana is a piece of Roman countryside. Thank goodness it has been neglected, you might say. If you pass through on foot or by car, along the part-surfaced roads, it is likely you will come across a fox or a family of wild boars; certainly, flocks of sheep crowd around the drinking troughs, jostling for position on September days still roasting in 35-Celsius summer heat. There is at least a kilometre between one farmhouse and the next; the human presence is transient, negligible. Some people have built themselves a villa, set up an *agriturismo* business or a farm. But the Marcigliana is the best place to forget about civilisation or even that you are human. If you venture a little way out into the trees, following the dense

woods or the open ground, you can get to Monterotondo or imagine yourself in the world of pre-Roman mythology, teeming with half-animal creatures, satyrs, the legendary she-wolf. Totally neglected means, of course, that no one has got around to putting up signage for the paths, sealing off access for cars or setting the park up for urban tourism. But indifference is preferable to speculation. What should be here? Should it be built over like the areas that surround it? What is there surrounding it?

We can zoom out on Google Maps to the whole of the administrative district, Municipio III, which extends either side of the ring road. A population of 205,000, a city within the city, an area of 98.03 square kilometres (Milan covers 181.67, Turin 130.01, Bari, 117.39, Naples 117.27, Florence 102.32, Trieste 85.11 and Bergamo 40.16), 2,000 inhabitants per square kilometre – or 4,000 if you discount the Marcigliana.

Each *municipio* (district) is a juxtaposition of numerous neighbourhoods (a competition to list the names is a good way to demonstrate how good your knowledge of Rome is). Municipio III consists of Monte Sacro, Monte Sacro Alto, Tufello, Fidene, Villa Spada, Serpentara, Conca D'Oro, Città Giardino, Prati Fiscali, Settebagni, La Cerquetta, Smistamento, Villa Ricca, Sant'Alessandro, Cesarina, Bufalotta, Talenti, Casal Boccone, Vigne Nuove, Porta di Roma, Casale Nei and Nuovo Salario, each area of the city with its own defining features, a church, a neighbourhood committee, a sense of loyalty, a Facebook page with a heading like *You know you're from Vigne Nuove if ...*

So let's take a piece of the city as a microcosm of the whole: Cinquina, the former *borgata* between Bufalotta, Cesarina and the Marcigliana. You head out of the city through Bufalotta, under the GRA overpass, take the right fork along Via Tor San Giovanni and arrive in the middle of a little group of houses that look like one of those two-dimensional sets they use in Westerns. Cinquina is perfectly divided into three blocks: 1) the old part, built (yes, illegally) from the late 1950s on Saturdays and Sundays by eager former employees of the farms run by an old fascist landowner by the name of Mauli, on plots belonging to another landowner named Camilleri, who had no right to sell them because they were mortgaged, but he didn't bother to take any notice of that and sold them anyway to release them from those very mortgages; 2) the white-painted social housing, dating from 1986–7, in turn divided into three complexes, B, C and D, with peeling walls, railings either missing or covered in rust; and 3) the brick-built social houses, which are new, extremely new – in fact, the last of them handed over just a few years ago. Two hundred families catapulted here from all over Rome and beyond: Ostia, Boccea, Lunghezzina, Anzio, Rocca Fiorita ... There is even an experimental apartment building, a European pilot project with solar panels on the terrace to provide electricity and heating (a sort of Saint-Simonian utopia for the brave new globalised world, except for the fact that every time a screw strips its thread or a tap breaks you have to wait for a spare part to come from France).

Cinquina is a microcosm of Rome, a sample we can study in order to understand how the city has grown since the Second World War, ignoring its mayors and laughing in the face of their development masterplans. In Cinquina (not even eight thousand inhabitants, 'a sort of village forced to become part of the city', according to the parish priest, who even looks like a country curate) you can clearly see the three waves of development, when bricks and mortar rained down on the area. In the 1950s and 1960s many families arrived from Le Marche, Abruzzo, Molise and Umbria: Cinquina was the first land they found that would get them closer to the Aurelian Walls as they came along the Via Salaria. They built their houses themselves then fought to obtain running water, sewers, a bus service and a paved road. In the 1980s and 2000s, on the other side of Via Tor San Giovanni (the road that cuts through the neighbourhood like the one in *West Side Story*) the social housing sprang up. The retired builders and farm workers who grew up here killed off the fireflies that Pasolini wrote about with gallons of weed-killer and went on to send their kids to university, or at the very least bought them an MPV. Their hair and teeth have definitely been looked after by professionals, and now they use those healthy teeth to defend the little bit of status they have achieved, insisting that poverty is merely a memory and determined that their bourgeois image should not be undermined, even by asso-ciation. By association with whom? With 'that lot in the new houses', the ones who 'throw their rubbish out into the street', where 'a month ago they found two little kids playing with guns outside their houses'. 'Since they've been here we've been ashamed to invite people round. We always go over to our friends' houses.' 'Before they arrived the neighbourhood was peaceful, and then guess what happened to our peace and quiet?' To keep an eye on *them* ('Some of them are bound to be good people, 20 per cent maybe') they collect signatures, talk about a neighbourhood policeman, a local police station, and eventually perhaps the fascists of CasaPound or Forza Nuova will show up, as they did in Tor Sapienza, Torre Maura and Casalotti, shouting that the suburbs are a tinder box, that the foreigners and the Roma are the gunpowder and they're prepared to light the fuse (see 'Revolutions in the Suburbs' on page 103).

A few years ago I met Mona, an Egyptian woman, along with her Italian friend Angela and both their families. Mona, oval faced with a chador over her head and a long dress; Angela with short bleached hair and wearing a white tracksuit. They had become inseparable during years spent in squatted housing in Ostia, where they lived opposite one another, and their children (four plus two) formed a single brood, its official language a mix of Arabic and Roman dialect. Some of what Mona told me about Cinquina was in line with the rest of the neighbourhood's views ('There's nothing here; I'm not asking for a cinema, just a few phone boxes'), but in other ways it was the opposite ('I've had it with police checks at all hours; I need to sleep'). Whereas on the right side of Via Tor San Giovanni they were proud of their home improvements, here, on the left side, she was proud to have a home under the

social-housing scheme, which she had furnished in a Middle Eastern style; she was driven by the hope of social advancement, of her family becoming Romans first and then Italians. One youngster – a friend of Mona's and Angela's children, he must be grown up now – used to come every day from Ostia, fifty-two kilometres each way; his family had not been allocated a home under the social-housing programme, so after school – if he wasn't bunking off – he would get on a bus and change four times to visit his friend from the squat. After an afternoon playing ball in the foyer of the building he would smoke a couple of joints and then, not as out of it as he would have liked, plonk himself down on the back seats of one of the last number-86 buses to wash up at the Cinquina terminus, taking the sunset as his cue to leave.

When I think of Rome, of the spectacle of its failure, I don't think about films like *The Great Beauty* or *Bad Tales*, the crime series *Suburra: Blood on Rome* or the documentary *Sacro Gra* (see the sidebar on page 129), I always think about those two boys. In its first incarnation, the extension of Line B1 of the metro – which has been in planning for at least twenty years – was supposed to extend beyond the GRA to Bufalotta and as far as Cinquina; it would have served this city within a city of 205,000 people with four new stations: Cervialto, Serpentara, Bufalotta and Cinquina. In 2017, however, the plan (still on paper) was changed, with a new route (rail rather than metro) due to stop only at Vigne Nuove and the Porta di Roma shopping centre.

Porta di Roma is also exceptional: the largest shopping centre in Rome, one of the largest in Italy and indeed in Europe ... To put it in numbers: 18.5 million visitors a year and rising (the Colosseum gets

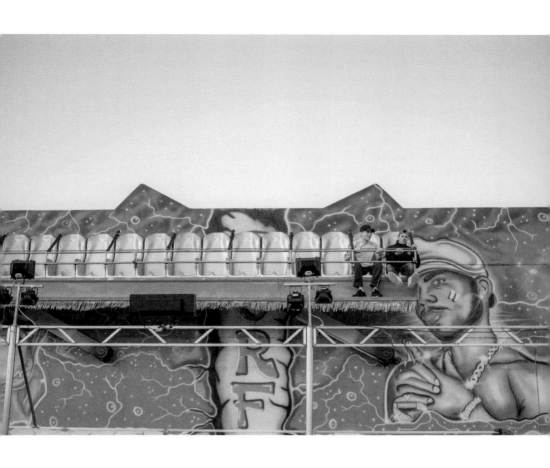

On the outskirts of Rome travelling fairs
are still a major attraction for young people.

thirteen million), with regular customers averaging two and a half visits each week and an average stay of over three hours served by a workforce of more than five thousand. All of this means that there are people who spend all day every day there: old people who come for the air conditioning ('It's better and more powerful than at Romanina'), childminders who leave the kids at IKEA's Småland play centre while they do their shopping at the Auchan supermarket, groups of twelve-year-olds who meet up there ('Their mothers are happy to leave them,' says the director, 'because someone's keeping an eye on them; it's full of cameras and security'). As well as the CCTV and hundreds of security staff, there is also pioneering surveillance software in operation: using a system of heat-sensitive cells, it checks for people leaving things lying around, people running and people stopping for too long in one place. Porta di Roma is immense, 150,000 square metres, a private city owned by a French real-estate investment trust and shopping-mall operator; in the original plan there were supposed to have been swimming pools, tennis courts and football pitches, but work never even started on those. Shopping brings more money in than a kickabout in the foyer.

And looking even further out on Google Maps, you realise that a section of the city appears to have been taken hostage. Decisions on what could be done there and how it might be changed are not in the hands of residents or their representatives but company boards, CEOs and directors. Less than a kilometre away, between Smistamento station and Prati Fiscali, is an inaccessible area four kilometres long owned by RFI – the state-owned company that manages the rail-network infrastructure – here, too, according to the 2005 RFI high-speed development model, there *should* have been a public-parks programme, but they were never created, and now the area is closed off even to pedestrians and bicycles. Opposite Smistamento station are two industrial facilities, one belonging to ACEA, the Roman electricity and water company, the other to AMA, the municipality's waste-processing company. The ACEA treatment plant fills the air across the neighbourhood with the stench of sewers. The former AMA mechanical biological treatment plant also poisoned the air for nearly ten years until it went up in flames on 11 December 2018. It has yet to be determined whether the fire was set deliberately, but the black dioxin cloud could be seen as far away as the coast. The area occupied by the plant was supposed to have been transformed by a cutting-edge environmental-redevelopment plan – a public park was suggested, a university, a satellite headquarters for AMA's management, a sustainability hub. Currently, as has been the case every summer or winter around here for the past ten years, all you can smell is the stench of the hundreds of lorries that park there with their rubbish fouling up the air of Villa Spada and Fidene.

RFI is a publicly owned joint-stock company, ACEA is 51 per cent publicly owned and AMA is a municipal company wholly in public ownership. How can anyone resist this legalised expropriation?

There has always been an internal conflict between the city's two souls: the spirits of rebellion and order, since the time of Remus and Romulus, Brutus and Caesar, Cola di Rienzo and the popes and the emperors. Rome invented the ideas of power and sedition. Despite the city having coined the very names and concepts of the city, citizenship and

The Insugherata Nature Reserve, between Via Cassia and Via Trionfale in the northern quarter of Rome, is considered the most beautiful of the city's protected areas. As is often the case in these parts, history and nature have come together and have even turned to legend: Nero's tomb is one of the major attractions, even though no one seems that concerned as to whether the tomb is genuine or not. This green corridor is home to over six hundred plant species, some of which, such as the deciduous woods, are very rare at these latitudes; the particular conditions of the Insugherata have allowed tree species that generally grow in cooler climates to have survived here since the last ice age, which ended around ten thousand years ago. The name of the reserve, meanwhile, derives from its star tree species, the cork oak (*sughera* in Italian). The regional body that operates the capital's reserves, RomaNatura, encourages visitors to bring a few corks with them so they can explain to their children where cork comes from, talk to them about recycling and 'teach them the importance of respect for the environment'. It is a shame the city authorities don't show the same level of respect. The reserve has two official entrances (and many unofficial ones), but one of them is barred by a metal gate and the other, on Via Castagnola, has been abandoned to the brambles and weeds, which make it difficult for humans to navigate the reserve's educational trail, although not the wild boar, which have proliferated and are venturing towards the main roads, attracted by the refuse. In response the authorities took advantage of the quiet of lockdown in 2020 to undertake a controversial blitz, in which they shot the animals with tranquillisers before capturing them, a practice that has been heavily criticised by environmentalists.

urbanism, to this day much of it is still not built on, with many areas untouched by human hands. If you zoom out on Google Maps from the Via Salaria to the GRA, you can see easily how Rome is a city that is resisting its own development, its auto-cannibalism.

In the year 0 Rome had a million inhabitants; in the year 1000, it was home to 35,000 people. It is difficult to live here but you survive. In 1973 it had a population of 2.7 million, and the authorities approved a development plan for a city that, it was projected, would grow to five million in the space of a few decades: the growth rate of a metropolis. Today there are 2.8 million people in Rome, just 100,000 more, but the volume of concrete has exploded. As a result of that development plan, suburbs were established that are now deserted and apartment buildings constructed that were left unsold and then unused. One such neighbourhood is Porta di Roma. It was supposed to have been the model of the 'new centralities', a euphemism designed to confer some prestige on outlying districts with no connections and no services – between the late 1990s and the early 2000s nearly twenty were built. Today families of wild boar saunter past shuttered or abandoned building sites. They are easy to find. From the shopping centre, if you take the viaduct over the ring road, it will lead you back towards the Marcigliana. Like nature's revenge or a welcome relief, the Roman countryside lies in wait. You're sure to come across a gate with a missing lock or a couple in their seventies in an old Simca who know where to pick wild figs. On the road that reconnects Tor San Giovanni with Via di Santa Colomba there are a few neat villas and an *agriturismo*, but otherwise it's fallow land with a few fruit trees, dirt tracks and half-ploughed

THE PASSENGER   Christian Raimo

Left: The Porta di Roma shopping centre (**top**) and the Mormon Temple (**bottom**) built by the Church of Jesus Christ of Latter-Day Saints in Bufalotta.
Below: A view of Villa Spada from the Via Salaria.

The Echo of the Fall

NORTH VS. SOUTH

The presumed rivalry and disparity between wealthier, more Lazio-supporting northern Rome and the more working-class, Roma-supporting south of the city has been transformed by television and social media into a running gag and source of clichés. Snobs vs. *coatti* (a somewhat disparaging word stereotyping a particular section of the working class), sushi vs. kebabs, smart aperitifs vs. beer and nuts, heading north on the Via Aurelia vs. south on the Via Pontina, the beach at snooty Fregene vs. cheap-and-cheerful Ostia and so on. Sketches based on the two hemispheres of the Roman brain are wildly popular, exploring northern and southern ways of celebrating Christmas, going to the gym and all manner of other things. And there's the inevitable TV series, Fox's *Romolo + Giuly*, in which an unthinkable marriage brings together two irreconcilable camps: the Copulati family of property developers from Roma Nord, and the Montacchi dynasty of Roma Sud, who are in the waste-disposal business. But how much truth is there in all this? Looking at the city in terms of the different points of the compass you realise that much of the population lives on the east–west rather than north–south axis, while GDP per head reveals more inequality between the wealthy north and the poorer east. So has the south been unjustly stigmatised? Maybe so, even though there is definitely a certain sense of southern pride, as illustrated by the rap duo Pippo Sowlo, who explain how life changes when you move from Prati ('Working metro, all very European / Rich kids, indie groups and lesbians at high school / That was how I rolled / Petit bourgeois parties, fascists and upper-class freaks') to Frascati in the south ('We went down to the jungle, bruv, on the south side / Social housing, *coatti* and ex-cons / Old men with no teeth, Arabs in a rage.') And the epilogue: 'You call it degradation, I call it authenticity.'

> 'On the road that reconnects Tor San Giovanni with Via di Santa Colomba there are a few neat villas and an *agriturismo*, but otherwise it's fallow land and a few fruit trees, dirt tracks and half-ploughed smallholdings. Does the city end here or carry on?'

smallholdings. Does the city end here or carry on? Is the fox crossing the road the intruder or are we the ones off our patch? Are the families of wild boar likely to attack or are they used to our human presence? And what about the buzzards and the porcupines? There is also a little group of fallow deer, they tell me, that probably escaped from some livestock operation. Have you spotted them? There is no perfect time of day to be here, but perhaps there is a better time, the time of surrender. Next to the handful of villas there are buildings of which only the skeletons remain, the steel cores of load-bearing walls, and old repurposed cowsheds, shelters for vagabonds or bandits, as well as the crumbling structure of the former asylum – five storeys of collapsing walls. It was closed along with the asylum of Santa Maria della Pietà. They used it to film the 1978 crime thriller *La banda del gobbo* (*Brothers Till We Die*) with Tomas Milian, and, in real life, it was where the Magliana Gang (see the sidebar on page 147) staged their first major operation: the kidnapping of Duke Massimiliano Grazioli Lante della Rovere.

In the 8th century BCE this was where the people of Crustumerium and Fidenae attempted to resist Alba Longa's war against Romulus. After founding the city, Romulus immediately went to war against the neighbouring peoples. That's right, there were other human beings before Rome, even if that seems an impossibility to natives of the Eternal City. Crustumerium and Fidenae were settlements founded earlier than Rome by the Albans. After the Battle of Fidenae, Alba Longa was razed to the ground and its inhabitants deported to the Caelian Hill, while Crustumerium and Fidenae were swallowed up. This was the strategy of *damnatio memoriae* and assimilation with which the Romans always tried to conquer the world, often successfully, a method they taught everyone who came after them.

And yet there is always something that resists this desire for obliteration. In 1970 excavations discovered traces of Crustumerium. What remains of the pre-Roman city is partly looked after at the Villa di Faonte (currently closed because of delays on the part of the government office), hidden between the back of the Matteucci Technical Institute and a discount supermarket; some of it has been brought inside the Porta di Roma shopping centre, where the director has set up a tiny archaeological exhibition ('The only museum in the world inside a shopping centre,' he boasts), and part of it is in the Marcigliana Reserve, right in the middle, not far from the two water troughs that are often surrounded by flocks of sheep, in the centre of a no man's land. A perfect spot in which to get lost and enjoy life. 🐟

The Family

The Casamonica clan is a network of Roma families that established themselves on the outskirts of the metropolis, where they thrived in the social and institutional desert, engaging in loansharking, extortion and drug dealing. Their empire, built on brutality with impunity, glories in the aesthetics of violence that are reproduced in the stories of the capital's underworld, in an open city that too often looks away as local mafias and international drug dealers mingle with entrepreneurs and politicians to clean up their image and launder their cash.

FLORIANA BULFON
Translated by Deborah Wassertzug

The entrance to one of the
Casamonicas' villas in Romanina.

They call themselves 'the Family Casamonica' (using the English word family rather than the Italian *famiglia*), their name surrounded by a logo of stars carved into the entrance of their lavish villa. They cruise around in black Ferraris sporting gold crucifixes and Rolexes with faces that complement their trainers. Their favoured model is 'Eye of the Tiger', which matches their colours perfectly: gold, with an animal-print face. A piece of precious metal worth $140,000, always convertible to cash.

In Rome crime has always told its own story, one that has been amplified by books, films and television series. The Magliana Gang became the subject of a well-known crime novel by Giancarlo De Cataldo, *Romanzo Criminale* (Atlantic, 2015), which was also turned into a film and a television series. Then there was the Mafia Capitale, which inspired the *Suburra: Blood on Rome* television and film franchise (see the sidebar on page 54). The Casamonica story offers a ready-made screenplay that sits halfway between the ragamuffin thieves of Pier Paolo Pasolini and the Romany gang in the BBC television series *Peaky Blinders*. It encompasses both rundown shacks and luxury, extreme poverty and high class.

Casamonica is a surname that no one in 'their' neighbourhoods dares say out loud, because it stands for fear. They are evil thugs with whom one does not mess. They threaten to break legs, and they beat people to death. They take starring roles in a metropolis that bows its head before a family that derives its power from meting out violence, threats and cash.

A Roma crime organisation composed of a clan of thousands who intermarry with each other, they are an empire that has expanded throughout the southern fringes of the capital. These people – carnies and horse farmers in origin – transformed themselves into scoundrels. They have built a web as strong as a mafia that is cemented by family ties, and they are able to negotiate with other criminal organisations who acknowledge their status, their territorial control and their ability to diversify their business and establish important networks.

No one enters their fortresses without permission. They decide which drugs to buy and sell and how high the interest rates should be on loans. To their victims they are 'sewer rats' – invisible until they pop up above the surface but capable of devouring anything and everything. 'They eat you. There are so many of them. So many brothers and cousins all around,' says a Calabrian, terrorised in spite of his connections to the 'Ndrangheta.

Rome's Wild West is their natural habitat. As you move away from the Colosseum and cross the ring road you encounter an enormous free port with

FLORIANA BULFON is an investigative journalist who writes for *L'Espresso* and *La Repubblica* and is a correspondent for Rai as well as international media organisations. She specialises in covering organised crime, particularly in Rome, as well as international terrorism and cyber-security. She is the author of *Grande raccordo criminale* (Imprimatur, 2014), which describes the Mafia Capitale system in Rome. She also made the documentaries *Invisibili* and *Vite sospese* and is a winner of the Carlo Azeglio Ciampi Schiena Dritta award, the Marco Luchetta International Press award and the Paolo Giuntella award. In 2019 she published *Casamonica: La storia segreta* (Bur) about the rise of the Casamonica clan, following which she found herself on the receiving end of threats to her life.

'There are hordes of brothers and cousins who intermarry and create blood bonds that recall the structure of the 'Ndrangheta. They are women and men who are ready to come together when the occasion demands but also to disperse – like a swarm.'

an absentee state and no rules. The clan is the only law. They live on the outskirts, and they know that Rome has entirely lost its centre. They prosper there, beyond the reach of the authorities. They dominate the darkest twists and turns of the streets of Rome, and the Eternal City is just territory to be conquered. Want an extension on the house? They build over the pavement. New car needs more garage space? They move the bus stop. No one objects.

*

They arrived from Abruzzo and Molise in the 1970s, putting down roots in Vermicino by the Catacomb of St Zoticus at the foot of the Castelli Romani and under the arches of the ancient Felice Aqueduct, in which, in the early post-war period, those displaced people photographed by Henri Cartier-Bresson made their homes. There, in the shadows of the ancient arches that are hidden behind fences topped by lions, they built a fortress. Porta Furba is a few metres from the Italian mint, the Istituto Poligrafico e Zecca dello Stato. Armoured trucks filled with banknotes drive past the castle where the Casamonicas take all their decisions, their money hidden in the walls and nine-millimetre 'irons' buried in the garden. Theirs is a violent criminal ascent proceeding amid housing blocks and urban sprawl and tolerated by a capital city that has become ever more resigned and fearful.

At first they concentrated on luxury cars and horse trading, a passion evidenced by the golden horses with Swarovski-crystal eyes that fill their houses. This is the style in which Uncle Vittorio grew up; he was celebrated as the 'King of Rome' with a triumphal funeral on 20 August 2015, a public celebration of his authority. This tribute went beyond the city limits and wound up in newspapers half the world over. The black carriage drawn by six horses was the same one used for the funeral of Totò (Antonio De Curtis, an Italian actor nicknamed 'the Prince of Laughter'). It was followed by a procession of Ferraris and Rolls-Royces that slowly rolled down seven kilometres of Via Tuscolana, tracing the territory of the family's expansion and finally arriving at the finish line: the large white Church of St John Bosco, which was the backdrop to Pier Paolo Pasolini's *Mamma Roma* and also where the funeral of Magliana boss Enrico 'Renatino' De Pedis was held. On the façade there were banners depicting Uncle Vittorio, dressed in papal white with a crucifix on his chest with the Colosseum and the dome of St Peter's in the background. As the coffin exited the church, petals rained down upon it, dropped from an unauthorised helicopter circling above. The band played the obligatory theme from *The Godfather*. Death becomes reality show, a consumer product to show off the glitz of power. Uncle Vittorio was not just a king to the Casamonicas – he was a pope, as good

Left: A villa belonging to the Di Silvio clan, home to those involved in the beating of the owner of the Roxy Bar and a disabled customer in Romanina.

Right: The entrance to one of the Spada clan's homes in Ostia. The Spada family live in social-housing complexes and mark the entrances to their homes with statues of horses.

Left: The entrance to Nando Casamonica's villa. The gates of the Casamonicas' homes are often adorned with the initials of the Casamonica and Spada families, marking the link between the two clans.

The Magliana Gang, formed in 1975, was the first criminal organisation to unify the Roman underworld, coordinating activities ranging from kidnapping to gambling and robberies to drug trafficking. Allied to mafia organisations, the gang also had links to neo-fascist militants, the secret services and high-profile politicians. Internal feuds, the evidence of supergrasses and a maxi-trial in 1995 put an end to their activities, even though certain members – in particular Massimo Carminati – reappeared years later in the Mafia Capitale investigation. In the meantime, however, the gang became the stars of a highly successful period for Italian TV. The magistrate Giancarlo De Cataldo told their story in his 2002 novel *Romanzo Criminale* (Atlantic, 2015), which was later adapted as a film and a TV series, both of which received great critical and public acclaim in Italy and elsewhere. The production company behind these successes was Cattleya, which applied the same model of adaptation for cinema and TV to De Cataldo's subsequent books *Suburra* and *La notte di Roma* (Europa Editions, 2017 and 2018, written with Carlo Bonino). *Suburra: Blood on Rome*, a prequel to the books and the film, loosely based on the Mafia Capitale investigation, was the first Italian series financed by Netflix, resulting in a kitschier, more grotesque but also more clichéd portrayal.

as Pope Francis, even though he more closely resembled John Paul II.

The family's rise in the 1970s was down to Enrico Nicoletti, treasurer of the Magliana Gang (the character Secco in the television version of *Romanzo Criminale*). He is the one who gave dignity to the Casamonicas in the underworld. He used them to collect debts, which produced revenue for him. They started off as unskilled strongmen but soon progressed to extortion, loansharking and drug trafficking on their own account. The Casamonicas do not have a *capo dei capi* but are organised into families: Vittorio, the patriarch, Giuseppe (aka 'Bitalo'), Guerino (whom everyone calls 'Pelé') are the best known and most dangerous. There are hordes of brothers and cousins who intermarry and create blood bonds that recall the structure of the 'Ndrangheta. They are women and men who are ready to come together when the occasion demands but also to disperse – like a swarm. This is the basis of their power. 'Our family is united. Our race is just made that way,' they explain.

They don't need to shoot anyone. They prefer fists to pistols and shotguns. Their strong arms are their heritage. They know how to hit hard. Some are professionals and prizefighters, like Romolo Casamonica, who competed in the Los Angeles Olympic Games in 1984 then wound up in jail for extorting a breeder who had sold him two chihuahuas. There are many brilliant stories of Roma and Sinti boxing champions. Those stories of transcendence are twisted by the Casamonicas into tales of cruelty and abuse. As with anything that pertains to Romany culture, they distort it. They are capable of whipping a young disabled person with a belt just for criticising a stupid stunt they pulled in a café and throwing bottles at a Romanian barista who has done nothing wrong other than not having served them first. To intimidate further, they roar off in a red Ferrari. That aggression, like the headbutting and clubbing they administered to journalists in Ostia in 2017, is criminal marketing. They are spreading their brutal message: 'We are in charge here. If you don't do what we say we'll kill you.'

They are a vortex that swallows everyone and everything, from social housing to the Café de Paris, made famous by the movie *La Dolce Vita*, where they might spend one evening suited and booted dining with powerful people and the next with South American narcos negotiating huge drug deals. This is a ferocious world that has grown unchecked and a city that hides everything under a veil. The Casamonicas are there, present but largely invisible. A family that is a lens focused on the virus at the source of the contagion infecting the heart of the capital. There is none of the ignorant innocence of Ettore Scola's *Ugly, Dirty & Bad* but rather they have all the trappings of a mafia. Children of a lesser god, they have forced their way in and become role models in a city where degradation and corruption are the system.

Both VIPs and unknowns line up to be received by them. It is an X-ray of a part of the city that falls into their web, with no distinctions between social classes or reputations. Illustrious victims, like the adopted son of Franco Zeffirelli, shopkeepers, entrepreneurs and other poor so-and-sos. People around whose necks they tighten the noose, people who become subjugated for life out of fear. Either you repay them immediately, at exorbitant interest rates of up to 1,000 per cent, or you become their slave. Otherwise it's a beating. No one goes to the police. 'They are animals, they dismember people ... I wouldn't give them up even if I were tortured,' says one young victim. They are intimidated, terrorised and roughed up, but, given a choice, they prefer the Casamonicas to the state. Instead of reporting them to the police they inform the family on investigations that are under way.

Loansharking is not only a source of revenue it also turns the family into a holding company. The clan has managed to take control of restaurants, cafés, bars and beauty spas. Some are just a few metres away from the Campo de' Fiori, the heart of the city's nightlife. Meanwhile they plead poverty and declare no earnings, like so many destitute have-nots whose combined assets are estimated to be €100 million ($117 million), hidden in trusts and overseas banks.

Cruel and ruthless, they flaunt their status by breaking rules, and they are often the only authority. In working-class suburbs they scoop up public housing, even deciding how it is allocated, but they don't live in it so they can avoid having to mix with *gadjos* (non-Roma). At a push they might take up residence there to hide in the event of police searches and arrests. And, as they do this, they obtain and retain approval by maintaining order in the housing units and offering work to those who live there. They can run drug-dealing hotspots, as seen in the Italian TV series *Gomorrah*, complete with lookouts surveying the streets and pushers on the payroll. But at the same time they can blend in and be involved in business, laundering both their image and their money thanks to professionals – lawyers, accountants and notaries – all of whom facilitate their connections and help them invest and wash their money in the city centre.

They took up residence at the margins

HOLLYWOOD ON THE TIBER

The Cinecittà film studios were established in 1937 beside Via Tuscolana in what was, at the time, open countryside. The so-called 'dream factory' began operations during the fascist era and went through many ups and downs, including being bombed by the Allies and raided by thieves and the Nazis. During the liberation of Italy it became a vast reception camp for refugees; five thousand people were still living there in 1951, and they found themselves employed as extras during the filming of the Hollywood historical epic *Quo Vadis*. In spite of issues linked to post-war shortages, the studios offered foreign producers a highly skilled workforce at a very low cost. In the 1950s and 1960s Cinecittà became 'Hollywood on the Tiber'. It was the golden age for films set in the ancient world, from *Ben Hur* to the legendary shoot of *Cleopatra* in 1963. Italian cinema was also developing in tandem, and Federico Fellini became the undisputed king of Cinecittà. But in the 1980s the Italian industry suffered a crisis, accompanied by the arrival of commercial television, resulting in financial difficulties (in 1997, on the verge of bankruptcy, the complex was privatised) and diversification: Cinecittà hosted the 1991 Eurovision Song Contest as well as a number of TV programmes, including the talent show *Amici* and the reality series *Big Brother*. In 2017 it once again came under state control, administered by the Luce-Cinecittà Institute. Major international productions never stopped, however – Martin Scorsese, Wes Anderson, Mel Gibson and more recently George Clooney are just some of the directors who have made films there – and have been joined by popular TV series such as Paolo Sorrentino's *The Young Pope* and *Suburra*. Since 2011 the studios and a number of sets have been opened up to visitors.

'It almost feels like walking on to the set of the Savastano house in *Gomorrah,* but the Casamonicas are not the imitators – if anything, they are the source material.'

of the metropolis, and when the city overflowed into their territory they became the rulers of new neighbourhoods that had no piazzas and too many shopping malls. Social desertification made them key players. Their money and their power won them acceptance from the *generone* – that hard-to-define Roman social class with an insatiable appetite for moneymaking – by bringing together the middle and upper classes and aligning them with the Casamonicas by their least common denominator.

*

The villas they inhabit could be out of a catalogue for the new criminal style, with busts of Julius Caesar (to make them feel like kings of Rome), satyrs, emperors and the *Bocca della Verità*, Rome's 'Mouth of Truth', rendered in marbled cement, the material of illusions. There is Venetian plaster, gold knobs and a silver-plated statuette of a Roman centurion commanding a chariot that is placed on the inevitable doily so as not to ruin the Baroque table. Champagne? They don't keep it in the cellar. They line up dozens of bottles of Veuve Clicquot St Petersburg in an illuminated glass showcase in the living room, alongside archaeological finds smuggled by grave robbers. Then there are life-sized ceramic tigers and panthers next to Padre Pio, a simple saint beloved of the humble who stands out in the hagiography of the clans and is venerated next to a case of profane knick-knacks, Fabergé eggs, Ming vases and thrones. Everything has the sparkle

of nobility, there as a way of forgetting extreme poverty.

It almost feels like walking on to the set of the Savastano house in *Gomorrah,* but the Casamonicas are not the imitators – if anything, they are the source material. The golden frame around the television was a family tradition well before they arrived at Casal di Principe, the notorious hub of organised crime in Italy. All that damask and gold recalls Russian affluence. They celebrate stucco and bling and precious stones. Everything must sparkle. Gold – *slato* in the Romany language – dominates. It is a talisman that chases away anything evil. It is used to upholster the cribs of newborns and even for toilets. The solid-gold toilet seen in the artwork *America* by Maurizio Cattelan, which made a splash in the Guggenheim Museum in New York, is routine for the Casamonicas, even installed in the Tor Bella Monaca housing estate. A golden toilet fitted with bidet can be ordered from a Naples-based company: just over $2,300 with free shipping. Then there are the iconic marble columns, symbols of imperial dignity, found in the kitchen, which resulted in court proceedings because, when an Iranian artisan refused to deliver the work free of charge, they beat him senseless.

They play themselves in crime dramas, and they are actors who are quick to proclaim their innocence on TV talk shows. Little by little, even the Cinecittà studios are being drawn into the perimeter of their kingdom. They're never shy of television cameras and feel no need to

Details of the villa confiscated from Guerino Casamonica, aka Pelé: one of the bedrooms **(left)** and a lamp **(below)**.

hide themselves away. Their look is widely imitated, and not only by young people in working-class suburbs. This is a source of pride to them. They flaunt everything on social media – particularly baptisms, weddings and funerals, which are funda-mental moments during which they stand together and make decisions on behalf of the family. Rows of custom-built cars assemble at villas and restaurants, where often they will not pay the bill. The women are dressed in furs and jewels, children in bowties and men in black suits with shirts open to show off thick gold chains. The menus feature lavish displays of seafood tartares and shellfish, paired with Armand de Brignac champagne – specifically a Brut Gold costing more than $2,000 a bottle and marked with the ace of spades, symbol of rapper Jay-Z. They especially love to photograph the cham-pagne with a pair of those gold Rolexes draped around the neck of the bottle.

They do not use credit cards. 'Their houses are full of money,' reveal Debora Cerreoni and Simona Zakova, two wives of clan members who had the courage to reveal the family's secrets. It is hidden

in walls, in skirting boards, in the oven – always available, good for catering to their glamorous whims and to make them feel like tsarinas. 'When they pay in cash it makes people happy!' Thus, according to Zakova, they come in from the outskirts of Rome to the Piazza di Spagna with rolls of banknotes. They receive invitations to fashion shows and are welcomed in boutiques with champagne. They have dedicated salespeople, and they buy entire lines of handbags from Chanel – perhaps because the double-C logo recalls the initials of the family name.

Women always take significant roles.

The Family

They make decisions, keep the accounts and pay doctors and lawyers. They keep drugs in dressing-table drawers in their bedrooms, but only during the daytime when their lookouts advise them that an unknown person is arriving, someone not authorised to enter their small fortresses. In the evening their job is to take the 'stuff' out of the house for fear of police raids. They also portion out the substances to be hidden in handkerchiefs, but only the craftiest ones do this. It is a delicate operation with no margin for error. They issue commands with the same ferocity as the men, and they are used to moving through stores as though it were self-service with no checking out at the till. They expect to take delivery of entire bedrooms of furniture or do the grocery shop, all without paying. They are matrons in bedroom slippers who yell at police officers. They are ready to defend their unauthorised castles from evictions or demolitions or to set up collection agencies.

*

The organisation of Roman narcos is a melting pot of separate tribes – much like the primordial Rome of the seven hills but banded together by a common interest, which is satisfying an infinite market. Rome remains an *open city*, like the title of the film that launched Italian neorealism. And Rome today is just as it was under German occupation: no armed groups and no acts of war. There is an agreement in place in order to avoid major clashes and to put business first. More cocaine is sold here than anywhere else in Italy – a disproportionate amount, according to data from the Italian Ministry of the Interior. Above all, however, there is investment here. In this way a medley of styles and methods has come into being.

The rules of southern Italy that demand that a single family be in charge of an area do not apply. Only the Casamonicas are able to negotiate with the elite of the 'Ndrangheta. They buy drugs at favourable prices from the notorious Strangio family, who were responsible for a gangland massacre in Duisburg, Germany, in 2007. They are buying ever larger amounts of drugs directly from the Colombians, using private planes and encrypted communications. The reality behind *Suburra: Blood on Rome* has turned into *Narcos*.

Every mafia needs a partner in the city, and they are the most reliable. They have cash on hand, they are immune to informers and their Romany language, which mixes with Roman and Abruzzese dialects, is difficult to understand. The few interpreters who can translate their intercepted communications are often threatened.

They are pleased by this nefarious fame: 'In Rome we are the strongest, we are mafiosi.' Their conviction has been iron-clad until now by their absolute sense of impunity. When it suits them they put aside their brashness and hide behind the victimhood of their Romany identity: 'We have always been persecuted. It's so easy to pick on us.' In their case, this is an excuse which has nothing whatsoever to do with the true drama of the Romany people.

They have managed to infiltrate the Palace of Justice, where they have sobbed, paid bribes, threatened and brought cases, thereby avoiding the harshest sentences. They have ended up spending part of their sentences in halfway houses where the practice is 'love as therapy and as a way of life' – a slogan that could be found on the wall of the establishment to which Bitalo was sent – in spite of their leading roles as narco-traffickers. They've even sent their lovers to seduce judges.

*

Over the past few years, as the Babylonia and Tempio 2014 anti-mafia operations have shown, Rome has become Italy's drug capital and is establishing itself as an international hub 'both from an operational point of view', explains Carabinieri commander Tullio Del Sette, 'with traffickers meeting in Rome to organise investments in cocaine and interfacing with the South American cartels, and from an economic point of view, because they are choosing it as the main platform for money laundering'. Bars, restaurants, cake shops, tobacconists and amusement arcades, dozens of these businesses are used to deal drugs but above all as investments through which to wash money. The new scale of the operations is down to the success of the local criminal set-up, which modelled itself on the 'Ndrangheta and the Camorra before setting up independently, although the southern-Italian clans retain the role of intermediaries, entrusting the Romans with distribution to the city's dealing sites. Over a hundred of these have been recorded in the investigations: from night-life hotspots to areas further out towards the edges of the city that follow the so-called 'Scampia model', where dealers – who can earn 'salaries' of up to €6,000 ($7,000) a month – are accompanied by lookouts. The Roman criminal underworld is more modern and fluid than the southern Italians, who remain wedded to bonds of honour and tradition. Cocaine is everywhere, partly through greater access following the collapse in prices, with the cost of a hit falling to around €20 ($24), less than a quarter of what it cost a decade or so ago, although after the outbreak of the pandemic prices bounced back up to €30–40 ($35–47). With bars and restaurants closed, the underworld adapted to the new circumstances to meet growing demand during lockdown, offering home deliveries: pizza and coke for the perfect night in.

Now, however, their famous impunity has been challenged. The Rome district attorney's office pieced together all the fragments of their criminal galaxy, and in July 2018 it challenged their organisation for the very first time. Several unauthorised villas were knocked down in a made-for-TV display that showed a number of ministers standing near the bulldozers.

It took two women, two *gadjos*, foreigners who entered the family but were never fully accepted, to snitch on them from the inside and rise up against their isolation and punishment in order to collaborate with the judges. It was only the courage of these women, as in the case of some 'Ndrangheta gangs, that brought about the collapse of a criminal system that had seemed untouchable. This is the end of the Casamonicas' tale, because, as the Sinti legend goes, 'The angels of destiny are received with all of the honours, and with a table set with three cups, sweets and wine, this last being replaced by water where necessary. But it is to these women of destiny God Himself has assigned the task of immutably securing the destiny of men.'

Now the Casamonicas have been wiped out in their prime, their properties and assets sequestered. Everyone applauded the district attorney's intervention and praised law enforcement. 'About time,' came the cry of relief. Then people turned their heads again, abandoning large sections of the metropolis to their fates without any institutional intervention to re-establish a sense of day-to-day legality. This is precisely what the Casamonicas and their emulators want. They are just waiting for the silence to return to reassert their authority. ◄

Ambitionz as a Roman: Trap from Trastevere

Hanging out on the border of Monteverde and Trastevere on a flight of 126 steps, a group of kids from central Rome began to make music, achieving national success with their songs about alcohol, drugs and their dysfunctional, hopeless lives. These personal, apolitical stories grew out of the imported sounds of trap, forming part of a nihilistic Roman tradition that describes a city without class consciousness – or, perhaps more accurately, a city that is a social class unto itself.

FRANCESCO PACIFICO
Translated by Oonagh Stransky

The Tamburino Steps.

If we were to think like publicists or travel agents or in terms of story-telling for a podcast, this would make a great story for tourists. On the border of Trastevere, on a steep 126-step staircase, a crew of rap artists was born. It's easy to get to the Steps. Starting from San Calisto, the bar directly behind Santa Maria in Trastevere where Lovegang go for their Camparis and Peronis, you cross Piazza San Cosimato, and in ten minutes you're at the foot of the Tamburino Steps, which were named after a boy who was shot down as he defended his city from the French while shouting 'Viva Roma'. The 126 steps, which give their name to the 126/Lovegang crew, rise up between buildings of diverse styles and end under an elegant canopy of trees typical of a bourgeois neighbourhood.

There's not much for tourists to do once they get to the Steps, though. It's just a place where a bunch of Roman musicians have been hanging out since secondary school. 'We sat there drinking, watching time go by / it never seemed to pass,' Franco126 sings. At this point the tourists ought to start imagining a group of teens, only boys, sitting around – beer, spliff, coke, crack – writing broken rhymes about heartbreak and breakdowns.

People who work in the universe of rap these days do their own storytelling and manage their own epic stories and multi-layered brands, making a writer who wants to tell that same story from an objective, authoritative and elegant point of view sound more like a news presenter. Nothing can be evoked to explain Lovegang's lyrics better than the lyrics themselves. You can only recite them; you can't understand them better than the person who wrote them. 'I'm always talking about drugs because that's all we do / I don't have content coz I'm empty inside / She thinks I'm cute / But she doesn't know that I suck / I cry on the inside and laugh / I'm buying this villa in Ostia Lido.' That's by Ketama126. His contribution to the genre is to talk about how he spends money, about success and to add sexist comments to twist the cold indifference of trap into folksy satire and slapstick through self-deprecating humour – like the wrong kind of beach house or general insecurity. A spark of life in a grim genre.

Lovegang is a group of kids who were born in the early 1990s and grew up in and around Trastevere, a touristy area across the river from central Rome that borders one of the city's most famous residential neighbourhoods, Monteverde – a district straight out of a Nanni Moretti film, whose emblem could easily be a tray of cream-filled pastries wrapped up with a ribbon for Sunday lunch. From this blend of street and salon, a scene was born: first came the 126 crew, with Franco126, Asp126, Drone126, Ugo Borghetti, Pretty Solero and Ketama126, then came the extended, more fluid version, Lovegang, which includes

FRANCESCO PACIFICO is a Roman author whose first novel, *Il caso Vittorio* came out in 2003 (minimum fax). Since then he has had a number of titles published in English, including *The Story of My Purity* (Farrar, Straus and Giroux, 2013 [USA] / Penguin, 2014 [UK]), *Class* (Melville House, 2017) and *The Women I Love* (Farrar, Straus and Giroux, 2021). He founded the magazine *Il Tascabile*, writes for *La Repubblica* and for the US magazine *n+1* and hosts a podcast, *Archivio Pacifico*, for which he interviews celebrities. He has also translated the work of numerous English-language authors into Italian, including F. Scott Fitzgerald, Kurt Vonnegut, Henry Miller, Dave Eggers, Hanya Yanagihara, Henry Miller, Chris Ware and Matt Groening.

Bar San Calisto, the centre
of Trastevere nightlife.

Carl Brave and Gianni Bismark. They first
made their mark on Italian music with
the double-platinum album *Polaroid* by
Carl Brave and Franco126 and the videos
for a number of singles that got millions
of views, including 'Rehab' by Ketama and
'Stanza singola' by Franco.

The idea that a rap scene could be born
in the centre of Rome takes us straight
back to the 1970s, to all the artists' studios
that were here, to people like Luigi Ontani
and so many others; a lifestyle that seems
out of step with the Airbnb era. With the
onset of the 21st century *il centro storico*
emptied out. It's now just a historical
theme park; no one really seems to live
there any more. And who knows what
kind of families the songwriters actually

come from? Maybe they're all rich or rent
out their grannies' homes on Airbnb. It's
hard to pin down just whose children the
musicians are. I know that one of them
has a father who's a journalist and another
one's mother is a professor. People who
run with the crowd tell me that there's
quite a socio-cultural mix.

Unlike the Roman music scene that
came out of the centre of the city in the
1990s – which had its headquarters at a
nightclub called Il Locale on Vicolo del
Fico (near Piazza Navona) and gave rise
to artists such as Max Gazzè, Alex Britti,
Niccolò Fabi and Daniele Silvestri – this
one, when it isn't trying to hit the charts
with the easier pop sound of Carl Brave
or Bismark and Emma, which is to say a
tamer version of popular domestic rock,
remains proudly insular and aggressive,
light years away from the sophisticated
Italian city-pop of its predecessors. This
is paradoxical, because the musicians who

From the Roma Sud exit on the motorway it takes half an hour on Via del Mare, traffic permitting, to get to Ostia Lido. Known for its dark sand, free beaches and polluted sea, 'Rome's beach' has always been an integral part of the socio-cultural history of the capital, even if Ostia, with a population of nearly ninety thousand inhabitants, has repeatedly tried to break away from the city of Rome, at least at an administrative level. Modern Ostia was developed in the 1920s with the construction of bathing establishments, including the celebrated Roma, which was later destroyed by the retreating Nazis. In the post-war period new bathing establishments sprang up for the Roman elite, such as the Kursaal, with its iconic diving board (rebuilt in 1997). A large number of film directors, from Fellini to Pasolini (whose corpse was found at the Ostia seaplane dock in 1975), chose Ostia as settings for their films. During the building boom of the 1980s Ostia became an important place for drug dealing and criminality. The Spada clan, who are linked to the Casamonicas (see 'The Family' on page 143), dominates the territory as the Mafia Capitale investigation revealed, leading to the dissolution of the governing body of Municipio X, which includes Ostia, because of their connections to the Mafia. Amid acts of arson in bathing establishments, shops and public buildings (for example, at the Building Permits archives and the Environmental Office), the summer club scene grew up, with discos and beach bars springing up everywhere and earning Ostia the nickname 'Coatti Beach'. With countless memes and viral videos that compare the 'authenticity' of Ostia with their cool, white-collared neighbours in Fregene, the 'VIP beach', one of the many social battles between Roma Nord and Roma Sud rumbles on.

went on to perform at Il Locale really did start out as street performers, going on to create an almost excessively clean sound. (They, in their turn, were descended from an older generation of artists from a different part of Trastevere, the singer-songwriters who performed at the Folkstudio, a club born in the 1960s where American artists or Americanophiles performed and which in the 1970s became a base for such political or 'moral' singer-songwriters as De Gregori, Venditti, Locasciulli and many others.) Thus we have three different visions of central Rome. The people who frequented the Folkstudio saw the city centre as a gathering place. In the 1990s opening a club near Piazza Navona seemed like an undertaking for the better off; going to watch a band in the centre – in the days when people went to gigs in grimier parts of town at venues like the Circolo degli Artisti (aka the Velvet Club) behind Roma Termini railway station – was considered snobbish. In the 2010s, meanwhile, we find a city entirely geared towards tourism and a music scene created by young people born and bred in its centre. In addition to Lovegang, there's the Dark Polo Gang, the band that shaped the development of trap in Rome; they came from another gentrified neighbourhood, Monti, and were druggy kids from other wealthy families. (Side, the most notable among them, is the son of screenwriter/director Francesco Bruni.)

Putting aside these socio-economic considerations, what remains is that tourists would want to go to the Tamburino Steps to witness something 'authentic', a real art form that counterbalances the trattorias, buskers, dossers and junkies: the Real Rome. Tourists see Rome as some kind of pensionless old man playing the guitar and singing songs for a few pennies.

'Rome has never committed to being bourgeois, it has never espoused a northern, Protestant industriousness.'

But even if they did encounter someone sitting on the Steps, would they know what they had found? Probably not. Some of the kids look bourgeois, some downright poor, some look like junkies – but rich junkies or poor junkies? It's hard to tell. The worst-off looking of them, Ketama, is actually the journalist's son. Funny story: at one point his father pulled his sax out of the cupboard and headed off on tour with Carl Brave, another member of the gang. Franco126 looks like a contemporary version of the singer-songwriters of the 1970s with his black jacket, moustache and dark glasses (even indoors); he affirms that singer-songwriters used to sing about love and melancholy, not about politics. Ugo Borghetti, who may actually be the most talented of the lot, has the face of a decent guy who ends up in a desk job at Italian multinational oil company ENI, although he talks constantly about dealing drugs and doing time in jail.

Lovegang is the now-unfathomable Roman middle class. Actually, maybe it's the same old underbelly of the city. Rome has never committed to being bourgeois, it has never espoused a northern, Protestant industriousness. Even if Lovegang came into its own during the era of trap, contributing to the genre with a few rhymes about the struggle to make money – 'I could have been a dead junkie / instead I'm a rich junkie' Ketama says – it actually repels the commonplaces of national and international trap (which I'd summarise with a verse from Sfera Ebbasta, 'If you talk to your crew and don't

talk about money, you talk about nada', or in one by Quavo and A$ap Ferg, 'This is a real rap anthem / Fuck a bitch in a Rolls-Royce Phantom / Fuck a rich bitch in the bathroom') and creates a romantic cinematic universe on the subject of the emptiness of life in the 'hood. In short, while trap is always about how far you've come, how you made money, how you found emancipation (and here I quote Sfera Ebbasta again, 'At the bottom I learned how to make it without getting fucked / At the top I learned how to make it double / ... I watch my past become history / Glory, for the kids from the 'hood / when pa isn't home when they come back from school'), the Steps seem like the cool place to be. And yet, that's not actually the way things are now. Some of them (Franco and Ketama, for example) have careers, and then there's the complex combination of local pride with the simple fact that Trastevere ain't no inner-city Atlanta or Milan hinterland.

Ugo Borghetti walks around in shorts and Crocs and rasps about summer in the city, 'Who cares about the sea? I go to Asp's balcony and stick my feet in a pail / It's only noon and we've drunk the supermarket dry ...' He walks through the tourist district with a handful of change in his pocket, there's fried chicken and cases of beer from the discount supermarket at home, but, 'Fucked if you'll find me rotting on the beach / I'll stay in the city and sweat it out / ... Watching the asses and whistling at the blondes.' If trap music challenges orthodox rap by refusing to

Lovegang and a crew of artists have launched a clothing brand that's popular
among the young people who frequent Piazza San Calisto.

Above: Young people in Piazza San Calisto.
Below: Sean, aka Pretty Solero, one of the founders of Lovegang.

make perfect rhymes, Borghetti is beyond all that; he's only interested in telling dark, raunchy, quasi-neorealist stories in time to music.

There's a kind of hauteur in their emptiness, a mistrust for the great adventures. The elegant neighbourhood of San Francesco a Ripa, for example, which Google maps calls 'a place of baroque churches, frescoes and masterpieces', to them 'Seems better to me than the Maldives / Better than lots of swimming pools / After four in the morning they're all hot / Even if I never know what to say / I hang with a friend inside / and catch some rays in the AC ...' Romans boast that they've seen it all: *quando voi eravate ancora barbari noi eravamo già froci* (while you were still barbarians we were already faggots), as the saying goes.

Franco126, meanwhile, sings about the glass of life: full of alcohol and empty of hope. His idea of Rome is non-progressive and anti-political. 'Beer and cigarettes to start the day / In the piazza there's a guy with a guitar who can only play one song / ... My father talks about a different Rome, swimming in the Fontanone [the fountain on the Janiculum] / I stumble around thinking maybe I had one too many / Getting home is gonna be tricky.'

They don't all write like 1970s singer-songwriters or amateur poets about subjects favoured by Arte Povera artists. Pretty Solero and Ketama prefer to dialogue with trap, ubiquitous as it is, applying their own finish to the genre's violent topics, 'My heart is cold, icy / She takes it in her mouth, like a lolly.' In their version of the genre they make barroom jokes, 'Double dose of whipped cream, damn it's already melted', which is reminiscent of the old Roman drinking song '*Osteria numero mille, il mio cazzo fa scintille*' ('Bar number one thousand /

My cock is on fire'). Pretty Solero, who's named after a brand of ice cream, adds, 'Snowflakes, morning and night / We're always together, me and my blue bubbles.'

In short, these artists have managed to climb aboard the rap-renaissance train with all its commercial potential but still manage to bring a distinct, personal, Roman way of talking about things, one that was passed down to them both from the Folkstudio crowd ('You remember Lella, the rich one / the wife of Proietti, the loan shark', ran a 1970s classic by Edoardo De Angelis about a crime of passion) and from the early-21st-century rap of TruceKlan ('Sitting on the bed, so / Thinking about money, yo, that I don't have, no / I turn on the TV, see people with money / So I go to the bank, yo, grab the manager / Cutter in my hand, no messing / Go straight to the cashier and empty out the drawer'). Asp126 creates phlegmatic rhymes about an afternoon at the bookmaker's. 'Give me the money you owe Bebbo / Grey days with stray change / that wants to be spent at the bar ...' And in a song featuring Massimo Pericolo, a rapper from the north, Ugo Borghetti evokes the anxieties of the violent and disturbed rap of artist Metal Carter (from TruceKlan). 'I'm constantly anxious because I sell smoke / Don't speak to the guards, fuck them / I feel as if I could piss on the grave of the person who birthed me / set fire to the boneyard / I stuff myself with pills because I know how to hate / my thoughts are always violent, but I'm always calm.' Borghetti manages to speak to a sense of vulnerability; he plays the gangsta as if he doesn't really buy into the role, even when telling stories about things that really happened.

Seen as a whole, their lyrics form a rainbow-coloured palette of depressive states. In a song about a band member

Hip-hop arrived late in Rome. Just like everywhere else in Italy, it had its roots in the squatting community and was explicitly anti-fascist. In 1990 the Onda Rossa Posse released their single 'Batti il tuo tempo', one of the very first examples of hip-hop sung in Italian. Now seen as the precursor of the militant rap of Assalti Frontali, they tried to superimpose the expressive and violent vein of the most political American hip-hop on to the Italy of the Tangentopoli corruption scandal of the 1990s. Roman rap is not very different from rap nationally: both inhabit the gap between underground and commercial, between political and personal lyrics, the boundaries between which are often ill defined. Some rappers, such as Piotta and, later, Brusco, add a certain light-heartedness that is usually absent from Italian hip-hop. The most distinguishing feature of Roman rap artists is how they use language to talk about the life in the 'hood. The collective Colle der Fomento was formed at this intersection of themes and styles by Danno, Masito and Ice One (one of the first DJs, along with b-boy Crash Kid, to spread the sounds of hip-hop in Rome in the 1980s), and their debut album, *Odio pieno* (1996), not only put Colle der Fomento on the map but the Roman rap scene as a whole. In 1999 the song 'Il cielo su Roma' was released, and it immediately became the city's anthem. The first volume of the compilation *Epicentro romano* (1998) brings together the best of rap from the capital city. In addition to songs by Assalti Frontali, Piotta and Ice One, it contains tracks by other major exponents of the 1990s: Ak47, Flaminio Maphia and Cor Veleno, who went on to become the most important artists of the second generation.

who died young, Franco mentions three things which, taken on their own, form a kind of haiku. 'Under a dark sky we kick a ball against the wall / Trying to be insolent but you really were innocent / Rocking on rickety wooden chairs.' That's the magic touch. Insolent/innocent is reminiscent of boys who grow up on the street. Unlike the worlds described by Pasolini or the Atlanta trap houses, where drugs were dealt and the genre was born, their life of violence was co-opted by the middle class, as Pasolini would say. They've been tamed. Franco, whose mother is a professor, sings, 'I looked for money in my mother's purse / But found only trouble.'

Tourists will have a hard time finding this kind of stuff on the streets. The city streets are fake, good only for selling the product known as Rome. Everything that can be experienced in this music exists on another level, a level that's inaccessible to foreign tourists, that of the Italian language and Roman slang. It is ironic that we are able to distinguish the different accents of the boroughs of New York and what their lyrics mean, but tourists will never understand how Roman rappers think. That's just the way it is. Our folklore remains incomprehensible. Our lyrics need to be translated and deconstructed. You can't just stop at the Steps and take in the view, see the half-empty bottles on the ground outside the corner shop. This may well be a case of musical geopolitics.

*

To my mind Lovegang sounds like a mash up between imported music and nationalistic/ultra-local music. The native pride in the genre seems both authentic and mail-ordered: it's a hip-hop derivative and yet, in a strange way, it also has its roots in Britpop, the music that grew out of the cocaine-fuelled Britain of the early

1990s when bands sang about ordinary, low-income people, their ambitions, filth and fun, whether trashy, romantic or megalomaniacal.

Let's take a closer look at Britpop. In Rome the genre influenced fashion – trainers, tracksuit tops, jeans, fringed haircuts and Vespas – and promoted an urban way of doing things. The band that reflects Britpop's influence the most is I Mostri, whose principal singer-songwriter, Pietro Di Dionisio, went on to play the guitar as a touring musician for Franco126. Di Dionisio is a brilliant figure in the Roman pop scene. In 'Cento Lame' ('100 Blades', essentially a cover of a song by British indie-rock act the Fratellis) he paints a portrait of Rome that is a disturbing mockery of the centre-left's very proper interpretation of the city, a gaze that combines their sense of moral superiority with their terror of chaos, their snobbery and their desire for 'respectability'. 'This is Rome / so welcome, but I already know that tomorrow Studio Aperto will report / that the knives are back in town / ... Today I read in the paper that / in Campo [de' Fiori] three foreigners were knifed / When will this story end? / What will the Americans think ...' The irony in Di Dionisio's lyrics make him the first Roman bad boy in pop music. Another track, 'Camilla', begins with another cryptic in-joke, 'This cocaine / is truly the bane / Of people who have to get up / early in the morning.' It continues, 'If we go out tonight / Where'll we go to get drunk? / Just bring on the bottles / so we can glass each other's asses' and goes on without any kind of restraint, concluding, 'The 2010s have arrived / People are even more unhappy inside.' This is a very different kind of songwriting for Italians, where people tend to choose either civic discourse or intimate storytelling.

At times Roman wit can be as dry as British humour. I Mostri's songs make me think that they listened to a lot of Britpop and spent a great deal of time and effort over their lyrics, ultimately convincing Roman songwriters to create a kind of music that goes beyond a basic borrowing of styles and focuses instead on the detached and unashamed desire to say things that are neither highbrow nor lofty but moody and romantic, hooliganesque.

When we talk about the origins of Roman hip-hop it would be remiss not to mention the 2005 collective album *In the panchine*, where TruceKlan's marginally gangsta discourse plays about with hip-hop's mother tongue, English. 'In the Audi, too fast for polizia / Show me paletta, I disappear, Santa Maria' – following the pleasure principle, 'Try to copy, my mezzo inglese, that's the schema / Senza pena for the scena estrema il problema / You need some rima, fuck your disciplina.' Lovegang, too, reveals this same urge to write purely for writing's sake, without any smothering preconceptions.

I'm not talking about influences here but rather the preconditions that gave rise to Lovegang's discourse. There needs to be a subculture before you can hope to redirect Italian cultural criticism, which is shaped by a blend of centre and left-wing politics and a moderate spirit whose general pretext is that the goal of art is to advance society. *In the panchine* and the work of I Mostri are two experiments that describe Rome with brutality but that also make people laugh; their goal was never to edify.

A third – and important – strand is the work of the group known as I Cani. A project developed by Niccolò Contessa, who was considered an innovator of Italian pop at the beginning of the 2010s, the band dedicated their first album, *Il sorprendente album d'esordio de I Cani*, to the systematic

You can find these tracks on:
open.spotify.com/user/iperborea

The Lovegang brand clothing store.

Campare di Campari
Asp126 x Ugo Borghetti
2019

Pretty De Niro
Drone126 feat. Pretty Solero
2018

Rehab
Ketama126
2018

Polaroid
Carl Brave x Franco126
2018

Crossword
Franco126
2019

Ambitionz as a Roman: Trap from Trastevere

'Lovegang gives us a city without class consciousness – or rather, it's as if Rome were its own social class, made up of people who do what they need to do to get by.'

destruction of centre-left culture, the kind that feels both moderate and revolutionary, consummately decorous while simultaneously celebrating the avant-garde. In a society where an excessively heterogeneous cultural canon (the social movements of 1968 and 1977, folk, punk and the avant-garde) was adopted by the bourgeoisie through facile comments in the culture pages of newspapers and magazines, Contessa saw the need to tackle the cultural sensibilities of the centre-left head on. Song by song he deconstructs the cushy lives of well-off, dull, 'enlightened', tame and so-called 'creative' young people. He ripped apart the bored, passively monogamous couples of means. He destroyed the creative illusions of kids who go to see a shrink on their parents' tab. He railed against the contradictory value systems that were passively passed down through families, 'Shame on you / And your post-patriarchal collectives / You only always wanted to be the boss's girlfriend.' Ten years on their lyrics might even be considered 'red pill' or alt-right, but back then they sounded like a necessary raging against the rotten bastions of culture and privilege.

By circumventing cultural schemes these three strands have created a space for a poetics of romance, one that is distinct from the moderate-left's hegemonic hold, one that allows the artists to speak more explicitly about the nihilism of Rome, one that is neither reformist nor revolutionary and, finally, one that is made up of spontaneous post-ideological connections, because let us not forget

that Rome always gets covered up by the hypocritical storytelling of politicians and writers for film and television. It is in this space that we rediscover the work of Franco Califano. In 1977 this artist sang about the illusions of love as a refuge from boredom, 'That long hug makes the illusion last / You don't want to think it's just a fling / So you say all the right things at the right time / and you think it works, it's all fine / Yeah, sure, but then ... / comes the boredom / no, not joy, but boredom ...'

In 2005 he reappears, older but still celebrating his anti-political detachment of *guardai le tele con aria ironica* ('I looked at the paintings with ironic detachment') and still with a vodka and tonic in his hand. (As a side note, he wrote lyrics for the pop group Tiromancino, who grew up out of filth, cruelty and psychedelics and who found national fame and cultural relevance by artfully cleaning themselves up.)

Lovegang gives us a city without class consciousness – or rather, it's as if Rome were its own social class, made up of people who do what they need to do to get by. The middle class is now an unmanageable sprawl, a single caste founded on the ideology of money, 'gear' and a perpetual state of gloom. 'Just pass me a beer and a couple of Tavor / I'm a better person when I'm high and drunk,' Borghetti sings. This blurred state suits Rome; it's a reminder of pre-unification Italy when the only Italians were priests, aristos and plebs. Franco126 is obsessed with drinking; there's a bottle in every song. 'We used to drink Sambuca but didn't

want to', 'I've got more than a few bottles to empty', 'There's an open bottle, but this wine doesn't quench my thirst.' It's a sad and common way of drowning without even having to become an alcoholic; it's the paralysing anguish of being caught between the moral obligations of the middle class – getting married, starting a family, *doing something with your life* – and looming boredom or death.

In an online video by *Noisey Italia*, a spin-off of the magazine *Vice* dedicated to music, Ketama replies to some comments below one of his videos. A fan writes and asks why they don't try to 'find something positive in the shit you go through every day', that 'they' constantly look so high that they seem 'ready to join club27' (those musicians who died at the age of twenty-seven, including Jimi Hendrix, Janis Joplin, Kurt Cobain, etc.). Ketama replies, 'First of all, a big-up for club27 ...' He blows a kiss to those who've died and says, 'I'll be seeing you all very soon. Second ... it's true, artists die all the time, like fallen leaves in September ... Artists are delicate, they have poor health because they're sensitive, so they die easily ...' Later, when someone criticises him for rolling a spliff on a copy of *Mein Kampf* when *Mein Kampf* should only be used for 'wiping your ass', he replies, 'True enough. I use it only for rolling joints. It's not like I ever read *Mein Kampf* or anything, much less preach from it.' There's no explaining the difference between the genius of the first reply and the sloppiness of the second. Apathy and a desire to speak the truth can't be separated. Any poetry in the lyrics is light years away from those kinds of places where people nod quietly in understanding or where poets are handed laurel wreaths.

In a way it's too bad, because there are real poets among the Lovegang crew. I think of Ugo Borghetti's unforgettable image, 'Alone in my bed, a lump in my throat, I plan the umpteenth disappointment.' Or, 'I've spent my life devoted to Peroni, hustling, swindling and dealing / I've shook a thousand hands but not one has solved shit.' The image of a cluster of shaking hands is a punch in the gut, as is that of a person alone in their bed making desperate plans that are destined to fail. Meanwhile, songwriting awards go to the genteel centre-left.

The subtlest poet to descend from the Tamburino Steps, the very talented Asp126, sings, 'People tell me that my Gs are animals / that just don't know how to behave / I pointed out that / certain animals have the prerogative to be tamed / but humans shouldn't be.' To some of us this attitude will sound somewhat sinister, it'll remind us of a certain individualistic notion of freedom that can't be tied to any form of utopia and, on the whole, we don't trust people like that. But, how brilliant, 'Me, I'm eaten up by anxieties / you, you're eaten up by taxes.' 🐦

What We Talk About When We Talk About *Calciotto*

In Rome *calciotto* – eight-a-side football – is far more than just a pastime; in the 'least professional city in Italy' it is the most serious and competitive activity there is. You give all you've got on the pitch, make and break friendships, rip nails, tear ligaments, age prematurely but never grow up, you might even find work ... Whatever else happens, though, it's got to be eight vs. eight.

DANIELE MANUSIA
Translated by Lucy Rand

The latest generation
of artificial grass.

Rome is a sticky city; it clings to you with all its habits and its shortcomings, and you carry it with you wherever you go. Or maybe it's that Rome tucks a sliver of your soul in a drawer, waiting for you to come back and claim it – and I don't mean that in a romantic way, quite the opposite. It's an embarrassing thing that makes Romans – even adopted Romans – weak. Take H, for example, a French guy who has lived here for more than ten years but is about to move back to Paris. He's going to take an advanced course for audio technicians and says there are more opportunities there in that line of work. And his family is in Paris. His father is getting older, and the idea of watching a Champions League match with his dad fills H with joy ... so he'll be staying in France for a while. He doesn't say as much, but maybe he'll never come back.

The thing he'll miss most is playing *calciotto*, eight-a-side football. We've been playing together once a week for three years now, and after one of our last matches we are both feeling sad. Standing in the deserted car park behind a pitch we've never played on before, I find myself unsure whether our silence is one of those rich with meaning or if we're just tired from the game. The relationships that are built around football are allusive, filtered through competition and a vague spirit of camaraderie that we like to believe is true friendship. The pitch backs on to a side-street off Via di Portonaccio, but it is strangely insulated from the sound of

traffic. I thought I knew all the football and *calciotto* pitches in Rome, but evidently not. What else are all these side-streets hiding from me? On this late-summer's evening the cluster of wooden sheds that we change in before playing, lit up by single flickering light bulbs, remind me of the wooden huts on the beaches in Normandy. The caretaker, a portly man in his sixties sitting idly on a plastic chair pushing the earth around with his feet like a child, could easily be a fisherman resting before a night of pulling in nets from a boat. The darkness of the hill behind the pitch, a bit oppressive but of a deep blackness that bleeds into the lighter sky behind, could be mistaken for the sea. H laments the fact that nobody plays *calciotto* in Paris and even five-a-side is rare. 'I'll have to find some Romans to play with,' he says. Some *Romans*, not some *Italians*.

It's nearly eleven o'clock. H leaves, and it occurs to me that no one, seeing him riding off on his scooter with his white rubber flip-flops, would guess that he wasn't from Rome.

It occurs to me that Paris will never suit him.

*

I'm well aware that the effects of the climate crisis – the end of the world? – loom over us while scientists talk of a new 'era of pandemics', but I was born in Rome in the 1980s, in the middle of a long recession interrupted only by the odd brief and fanciful pause, and the two things I've seen start and grow big

DANIELE MANUSIA, the editor and co-founder of the sports magazine *L'Ultimo Uomo*, was born in Rome, where he lives and works. He has been a contributor to *GQ*, *Vice*, *Nuovi Argomenti*, *minima&moralia*, *Orwell* and *IL* magazine. He is the author of a number of works on football, including a book about the celebrated French footballer Eric Cantona, *Cantona: Come è diventato leggenda* (add editore, 2013), and a biography of former Roma star Daniele De Rossi, *Daniele De Rossi o dell'amore reciproco* (66thand2nd, 2020).

'The seriousness of the system is magnified, as in a fairground mirror, in the individual players and teams. They warm up, they talk tactics, they play to the death.'

enough to change my life and that of the people around me are the World Wide Web and *calciotto*.

They also play *calciotto* (*calcio*, football, and *otto*, eight; five-a-side is called *calcetto*, the diminutive version of *calcio*) elsewhere in Italy, but the seven-a-side format is much more common, especially in the north. There are people who find this particularity irritating: why do Romans always have to be different? *Calciotto* wasn't even a thing when I was thirteen or fourteen. You played eleven-a-side or, if needs be, with a variable number of players on the school or youth-club basketball court or in the park. Then someone had the good sense to make use of a full-sized pitch divided down the middle, like they do in amateur-team training when there aren't twenty-two players available. We played our first matches on the dusty pozzolana surface with traffic cones marking the pitch area and giving the games a relatively standardised shape. Then AstroTurf pitches started to pop up in a few places, a technology that developed quickly: the grass-like blades got longer, and the original sand was replaced with granules of black rubber, carcinogenic according to some studies, which have now disappeared (or rather, been reduced in size and are perhaps made from a different material, but we still have to tip it out of our boots after every match). Until a short while ago people still talked of third-, fourth- and fifth-generation turf, whereas now they've lost count and just say 'latest generation'. Many traditional football fields have been converted into sports clubs with one or more pitches, well-equipped changing rooms, bars and, in recent years, paddle tennis courts (the second 'club' sport for city-dwellers). The size and shape of the pitch also depends on the land available: some are long and narrow, while others are almost square.

These days kids as young as fourteen book the pitch for an hour in the afternoon. The spontaneity has been organised. It was not difficult for me to transition from the improvised games of my childhood to the very serious business of *calciotto* tournaments (as if the latter were the natural evolution of the former), with its annual membership subs and booking fees for the pitch and the referee. Those who organise everything are estate agents or building managers by day (only the lucky ones can dream of doing this full time) who top up their salaries by spending their weekday evenings on the field collecting money and checking everything is running smoothly, calling an ambulance if a ligament gets torn or an ankle broken and, when the situation calls for it, breaking up a fight. Every neighbourhood has its tournament, each with trophies for best player, top scorer and best goalie. Some have post-match interviews, a well-made website and teenage models who are paid a few euros to stand at the edge of the field before the final, with techno music blaring before the match and players walking out on a red carpet. The most prestigious, or at least the most popular, tournaments in the area even pull a crowd in the later stages.

Clockwise from top left: Lorenzo, an accountant, Flavio, a lawyer, and Alessandro, a doctor.

The seriousness of the system is magnified, as in a fairground mirror, in the individual players and teams. They warm up, they talk tactics, they play to the death. These tournaments bring out the worst in the players; one even wonders if that's the main reason they play. Sometimes well into their thirties, forties or even fifties. This might be why, at a weekly match in the neighbourhood of Tor Pignattara in which I once took part, generations of friends and family are thrown together in one big masculine melee, the younger ones dribbling as the seventy-somethings, glued to the spot, resort to a judiciously placed stud to the shin. Of course, you also see women on the pitch – in fact, in a five-a-side tournament between lawyers it is compulsory to have at least two women – but Roman *calciotto* is a male-dominated narrative, and so, inevitably, decadent and tinged with nostalgia. It is the song of a bygone youth, the cult of a type of man who nowadays exists only here, in Rome, on the *calciotto* pitch.

And how much longer will it last?

Like all cults, from the outside it looks insane. On more than a few occasions I've brought friends along from Milan or even Sweden to play, and they've all commented, either excited or terrified, 'But you guys are nutters.' In my head I have a map of Rome on which, instead of all the monuments and main roads, I've marked the city's *calciotto* pitches. I could organise tours. On the 'gold package' one or two tourists join in an authentic match between Roman teams. You'd get a complimentary Totti shirt and a temporary tattoo of the Colosseum. I've played with doctors, vets, waiters, journalists, writers, poets, sculptors, actors, warehouse workers, florists, builders, bricklayers, budding politicians, university professors, unemployed bums

and semi-criminals. Once upon a time it was said that you're not a true Roman male if you haven't done a stint in Regina Coeli prison. Today it could be said that you're not a true Roman man if you don't play *calciotto*. In the changing rooms you find work and strike business deals, you meet the right people at the right time, but you also put the integrity of your joints in danger and run the risk of destroying decades-old friendships. To find out whether there's a Roman *calciotto* player hiding under the bespoke suit of a respectable professional, perhaps with his accent camouflaged to do business in Milan and Turin or London and Paris, take off his shoes and look for crooked toes and black toenails. Or, if you get a chance to pull down his trousers, expect to find a scar on the outside of one knee.

Today there's an eight-a-side football championship in Rome that is more official than all the others, with a Serie A, Serie A2 and Serie B, and a total of 150 teams are signed up. *Calciotto* has been professionalised, which is a paradox for the least professional city in Italy. It is almost as though Rome has taken all the seriousness it can muster and poured the whole lot into amateur football. Once upon a time the top teams were Checco dello Scapicollo – a restaurant in Rome's business district with a huge garden where they held weddings and other events – and Cotton Club, an all-day restaurant-cum-lounge bar with live music in the Trieste neighbourhood. These days the top teams are Roma, Lazio and Totti – Francesco Totti's own team, captained by Francesco Totti, which won the last match of the tournament thanks to a goal by Francesco Totti (in the final against Lazio ...). And there's no difference in *calciotto* between a goal scored by Totti and a goal scored by my teammate.

Totti – first among Romans – has devoted himself to the pastime of the everyman, just like Emperor Commodus, comedian, gladiator and son of Marcus Aurelius, whose vices, according to British historian Edward Gibbon, 'cast a shadow over his father's virtues'.

Totti celebrated his forty-fourth birthday with a game of *calciotto*; his friends threw him a surprise party before the game, and he scored. Nobody represents the deeper meaning of Roman *calciotto* better than the legendary A.S. Roma player who just can't stop playing football: not to be able to imagine yourself without boots on your feet, without the pain of your own toes squeezed into shoes a size too small, confusing your own infantilism – rolling your own identity up like you would a banknote and slipping it down inside your football sock – with something epic.

Calciotto, with its perfect dimensions (a pitch that eight people can cover at a jog) and the perfect ratio between energy required and freedom of action, could be the sport of the future, with national and international potential. It's just a shame that Rome is only interested in Rome, past and present.

*

What is the opposite of *elegance*? We would usually say vulgarity, brazenly exhibited bad taste. But if by elegance we don't mean solely the end product that we see in front of our eyes – the grace, that is – that seems to animate certain people but also the way in which that particular elegance reaches our senses – with an apparent naturalness, as if completely effortless and unforced, as if it were an absolute, the very essence of that person – if we think of elegance as a quality that remains for ever inaccessible,

Rome has some of Italy's most fervent football fans, whose passion is so all-encompassing it's almost suffocating. Rome is a city obsessed with football, as the American co-owner of A.S. Roma, James Pallotta, soon realised when he arrived, saying, with a mixture of amazement and suspicion, 'It really is tribal and cultural, way more than it is in US sports.' Politicians need to be careful, too. During the 2016 mayoral race Virginia Raggi, to be on the safe side, hid behind an innocuous claim to support the Umbrian side Ternana, only coming out as a Lazio fan once she was in office. And despite having proclaimed his support for Juventus, the newly elected Walter Veltroni 'redeemed himself' by wearing a red-and-gold scarf at the celebrations for Roma's 2001 title win. The capital is famous for the power of its organised fans, who even forced a derby match to be abandoned in 2004 by spreading a false rumour that a child had been run over by a police van; the Roma ultras leader Daniele De Santis, who was later sentenced to sixteen years for the ambush of the Napoli fan Ciro Esposito, convinced Roma captain Francesco Totti to call off the game. Also in 2004 the city saw the launch of *Il Romanista*, the first newspaper in the world dedicated to a single football team. Then there are the local radio stations devoted entirely to Roma and/or Lazio – a football-related social phenomenon not seen anywhere else in Europe and which pre-dated the arrival of the social networks – that provide a megaphone for the voices of the ultras and broadcast an endless stream of inane barroom chat. Pallotta came out against these destabilising influences by setting up his own 'state' broadcaster to counteract them. 'There used to be nine radio stations talking about Roma twenty-four hours a day,' he said. 'We've got rid of two of them so far, there're still seven to go.'

The entrance to the Atletica 6 Sports Club on Via Latino Silvio, near Via di Portonaccio.

imperceptible, then we must find a more complex opposite than simple vulgarity. Whatever the word is, it is what guides Romans in their tastes and behaviours.

When it comes to Romans, nothing remains hidden from view. Perhaps because of a total refusal to indulge in interiority, Romans place importance only on external appearance; everything must be explicit, declared, visible. And, perhaps because of its difficulty in presenting itself to the world, Rome has nothing but self-image; the rest doesn't exist. On the shiny shin bones, the thighs and the forearms of Romans you find gladiators and ancient monuments, Latin script framing portraits of children and wives. They don't seem to be the result of an active decision-making process – go to the tattoo parlour, choose

the image, wait patiently while the needle completes the fresco, pay – but rather that time itself has left these marks on the skin of those who carry them, as if they were born with tattoos of ancient Rome. The gallery in which to exhibit them, it goes without saying, is the *calciotto* field. A celebration of Roman-ness among Romans.

Do Parisians tattoo the Eiffel Tower on to their skin?

The vast majority of the shirts on display – and the shorts, too – are those of the two Roman teams. Even in this, Rome's tastes are over the top; every fan is a superfan, there's no middle ground. It's a totalising and totally exterior, materialistic idea. Over your morning coffee you read only the sports pages that cover your team – with a caustic eye on those of your rival; in the car you listen to the radio station that talks about your team twenty-four hours a day; on the pitch you wear the sacred vestments: knee-high socks, shorts, shirt and, if it's cold, a neck warmer or hat in the appropriate colours. In Rome a person's love is made flesh, tattoos of wolves and eagles blaze, even more visible than usual. A Roman cannot keep anything inside, and he exposes more on the pitch than on the beach. Roman style is a form of self-celebration; even old injuries are commemorated with ankle supports or knee and elbow protectors.

But the pitch is also a place where you can express yourself in a unique way, where you allow yourself to stand out, albeit within pre-set boundaries. Rome fashion week takes place on the *calciotto* field, and every eccentricity is allowed. Twenty-somethings with Cristiano Ronaldo haircuts – cosplayers in shorts and the number-seven shirt, standing with their feet wide apart before taking a free kick – share the pitch with former semi-professional players rubbing camphor oil into their muscles, its pungent whiff heralding each of their moves, and men in their forties wearing the same tight shorts they had in their teens. You also see unusual shirts with regular names and dates of birth instead of numbers, graduation gifts with *con lode* (the highest distinction in Italian universities) written in place of a surname and the player number as 110 (top marks). Old, threadbare shirts play alongside highly sought-after ones and those of obscure players from far-off places.

Yet there is a strong undercurrent of conformity. It is a masked ball that wants nothing less than to overturn the established order, an innocuous carnival that affirms each person's place in the world in a purely reflective way. My hero, someone I envy and could never imitate, is a slightly odd friend of friends who turns up each week in a white cotton shirt he probably slept in the night before, wearing glasses and a bandana around his head that

The classic set-up is 3-3-1, offering 'the best coverage of the pitch'. No one gets too tired with two players on each wing, even though the central midfielder shoulders a lot of responsibility. Recommended for those who fondly remember Zdeněk Zeman's coaching style.

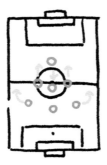

2-3-2 is an experimental formation for teams combining talented young players (who have to cover the full length of the pitch on the wings) with less youthful talents (up front). Few teams can allow themselves two strikers, and so this formation is only recommended for those with good technical skills, particularly in central defence.

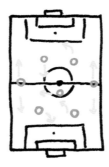

Clockwise from top left:
Nicola and Alessio, lawyers,
and Holle, an accountant.

makes him look like David Foster Wallace. In winter, when he wears thermals, he doesn't wear shorts over the top and runs around with his buttocks in full view, the shiny material pulled taut. It seems like he really wants to play, and he turns up without fail every week, but at the same time he evidently refuses to take this hobby seriously.

*

As I'm writing this piece I receive a message from V asking me if I want to take part in an over-35s tournament with him. I remember how when we were twelve I made him cry because he started growing a moustache before everyone else. Later we became best friends. I stayed at his house once every two weeks for at least three or four years. I've been on holiday with his parents. The first motorbike I ever rode was his. Together, when we were seventeen, we reached 270 kilometres per hour on a consular road. When we were at high school he was so bad at football that he would only play because he was my friend, and on the pitch I'd shout commands at him as if he were a dog I was training. But this constant bullying brought out the best in him, at least I think it did. He came to my father's funeral. I always ask him how his parents are even though, since we haven't been playing together in recent years, we've stopped meeting up. He's never met my daughter, who is nearly two, and, although I sent a card when his daughter was born three months ago, it hadn't crossed my mind to arrange for us to meet up.

My past melts into the turbid years of tournaments and those of matches among friends organised as if they were tournaments, scrambling to get two equal teams together, creating a hierarchy in my address book of who to call first because they were 'stronger' and who last, the 'lightweights'. Friends were cut out of the team without a word while others stopped picking up the phone because they already knew what I was going to ask. My past is full of people who will remember me exclusively for how I played football five or ten years ago, people I treated badly – in some cases very badly, shamefully – and others who will remember having shared profound moments with me. An excited embrace following a goal during a tough match, perhaps?

I feel ridiculous projecting any type of profundity on to *calciotto*, but I also can't bring myself to say that it's a superficial experience. I've devoted so much energy to it over the years that I refuse to consider it 'just a game'. There was a period of my life when match day was dedicated almost entirely to sourcing players to fill in for those who couldn't make it. I was working, of course, but only in the scraps of time that I didn't spend in the bathroom, corridor or huddled over my desk phoning a potential player. Before the advent of WhatsApp I had to phone one person at a time or pay for SMS messages: it came at a cost that wasn't just metaphorical. There's always someone who realises he can't play on the morning of the match, but there's also always someone ready to turn up at half-an-hour's notice, someone who runs out of the office, drives in the rush-hour traffic risking fines and accidents, quickly grabs his bag from home and gets to the pitch just in time to be welcomed like a hero. The best are those who always have a bag ready in the car, just in case.

Look at all the professionals in Rome – the lawyers, the accountants, the young notaries – who all seem caught up in whatever trouble they're having at work but really all they're thinking of is the nine o'clock game. Will they manage to beat the team above them in the table? Will they get past the quarter finals this year, or will it be another disappointing season?

*

When my time as a competitive footballer came to an end and my rivals started making jibes along the lines of 'Careful now, you're fifty, you know', I returned to those games among friends but still as a group of sixteen, eight vs. eight. In fact, I'm thirty-nine, but I still go around in summer with blackened big toes. My body is always stiff and lags behind my thoughts, but I keep on trying complicated things, things which were once *mine*. Nowadays I have to be careful what I eat for lunch on match day, and I can't go out on to the pitch with an empty stomach; the night after the match it has become harder and harder to sleep, still tossing and turning in bed at 1 a.m., and when I finally do manage to drop off I get woken up by cramp in my feet, calves or, the worst muscle of all, the most difficult to pacify, the tibialis anterior. Who knows, maybe one day *calciotto* will have made me an insomniac.

I no longer play with the people I used to play with, the ones with whom I shared the most competitive years of my life. I suppose you could say things ended badly. The very ruthlessness that has a positive connotation in football and that I believed served to keep my concentration levels and those of my companions high was served back to me all at once.

Suddenly, I was no longer good enough. I had become the lightweight.

There are, of course, tournaments for the over-forties, even the over-fifties, but these days I feel that it's no longer so important to have a consistent technical level. I've learned to contain my disappointment when a teammate misses a pass; I've even learned to accept my own errors – well, more or less. The pleasure of seeing the same people each week trumps the rest of it, and the matches are no longer torture when they don't go my way. The thing that matters most is packing my bag at seven in the evening and emptying it straight into the washing machine at ten. Perhaps the secret of *calciotto* is in the repetition, in the same gestures repeated over and over again, like mass or a Rothko painting. All part of an illusion of eternity and stability.

The other important thing is the psychic intensity of those hours, which lights up the senses. A moment before kick-off I find myself observing the landscape around me with new eyes; the pine trees that surround the pitch are illuminated by Rome's sunset like logs of wood in a fire; on a windy evening the bushes that grow behind the goal, bordering the fields, wave around like seaweed under water. In winter I find it wonderful to see my own breath in the air, feel the damp on my bare legs and realise that it's not another night spent on the sofa or in the warmth of a restaurant. After the match, as I drive down the eerily empty roads – the streets of Rome on a week night are deserted – with wet hair and the car full of the scent of body wash, I have the impression that my demons have been defeated, at least for an evening.

Roman *calciotto* is at once an autobiography and a polyphonic novel. It is a solitary group activity: we are all looking for the same thing on the pitch, but everyone is going it alone. In more than twenty years I haven't yet found this thing. There's something self-destructive about it, and even this is typically Roman. Otherwise, why not dedicate yourself to healthier activities? Why, instead of becoming joggers or delicate tennis players of the

Via di Portonaccio sports club.

sort who pass the ball back and forth over the net rather than searching for their opponent's weak spot, do we squeeze ourselves, nervous, through the evening traffic and cross half the city to put stress on our joints and minds? Why have we dedicated all this energy to a child's game? In what paradise do we think we're going to wind up when the end of the world begins, inevitably, in the place we believe to be its centre, Rome?

Whatever the reason, Romans keep playing. They can't help it. My brother-in-law, who is fifty-six, still plays with his childhood friends. The day after a match he walks up and down the corridors at work, limping showily because of a persistent pain in his calf. The limp gradually subsides in the days that follow until, a week later, the day of the next match, it's completely fine, and the cycle begins again. 'I started playing five-a-side on tennis courts,' he says. 'In the evenings they would take the nets down, but the holes for the poles that held them up remained. We would return home covered in red earth. Then they made the pitches synthetic, five against five, but *calciotto* is another thing entirely ... it's the closest thing to football. After fifty years your physique changes; you'll notice. The decline accelerates. I play with the same three or four friends that I always have. When I see them wearing shorts, the way they run for the first few steps as if their legs were made of wood, and then how they play once on the pitch, I recognise the boys they once were. And they see the same. Every so often I'll do something, dribble or shoot, and one of them says, "Oh, you did that just like when we were fourteen."'

DANIELE MANUSIA
Translated by Lucy Rand

The Newcomer

RARITY: ★ ★ ★

Unfortunately, as the years go by fewer and fewer players over the age of thirty come to *calciotto* for the first time.

SKILLS: ☆ ☆ ☆

Whether a player's never 'truly' played or has come from five-a-side, it makes no difference. It takes a couple of years at least to get used to the size of the pitch and the number of players in the opposing team. Sometimes the newcomer never quite gets there.

RISK TO (YOUR) KNEES: ★ ★ ☆

He is usually a decent guy but sometimes hasn't completely mastered his own body, which can easily be transformed into a weapon.

FRIEND POTENTIAL: ★ ★ ★

He is enthusiastic and hungry to learn. You can even use him as an object for stress release: just let rip in his direction on every possible occasion.

You can see straight away when someone hadn't played football as a kid. He'll turn up in a white T-shirt or, worse, a polo shirt. In the most hopeless of cases he won't even have boots, convinced that trainers will do the job. Wearing a watch and with a bandana around his head, he doesn't defend or follow tactics and is completely unpredictable on the pitch. As he learns to play he never loses the sense of unfamiliarity with the ball, which he struggles to control and kick properly. From time to time, however, the new guy can pull an incredible move out of nowhere, made even more beautiful by the element of surprise.

The Superfan

RARITY: ☆☆☆
They're the majority.
SKILLS: ★★☆
There are great ones and terrible ones.
RISK TO (YOUR) KNEES: ★★☆
He is capable of breaking you,
and himself, to honour the shirt.
FRIEND POTENTIAL: ★★☆
A simple soul who just likes to be part of
something bigger – as long as you don't play for a
rival team there's a good chance you'll get along.

Wearing your team's shirt heightens your sense
of responsibility when you play, but true fans
don't limit themselves just to the shirt with
the name and number of a favourite player (in
Rome, 90 per cent wear a Totti shirt) but also
socks and shorts emblazoned with the favoured
team's logo. Perhaps each item will be from a
different era: socks from the 1990s, shorts from
last season, shirt from the early 2000s when
Rome and Lazio topped Serie A and won their
last scudetto. Often has the name of his team
tattooed on one arm, not far from the names of
his children. He sweats through the shirt on the
pitch but is always careful not to damage it.

The Oldie

RARITY: ★★☆
More common on the pitches of Rome
than one might think, but usually playing
against others of a similar vintage.
SKILLS: ☆☆☆
He'll play for as long as he can stand but
will often stay rooted to one spot.
RISK TO (YOUR) KNEES: ★★☆
The need for vengeance against anyone who
manages to dribble past him has lingered since
his youth, meaning he is likely to tackle hard.
FRIEND POTENTIAL: ★★★
He may be no more than forty, but
he has a wealth of stories.

Beyond the age of thirty the oldie starts adding
to his kit, starting with an ankle support or an
elasticated strip that holds his knee together
and continues with a back brace or elbow pad. A
long warm-up before playing is executed, almost
in slow motion, as if the slightest increase in
speed could cause him to shatter into a million
pieces. In winter he sports gloves, a neck warmer
and, on really cold days, a hat, T-shirts with long
shiny sleeves made from a synthetic fabric that
has been out of production since the 1990s. He
still wears the same shorts he did at the age of
twenty, which are now tight around his thighs,
which rub against one another when running.
If it were up to him, he'd die on the pitch.

The Pro

RARITY: ★ ★ ★

Extremely rare. As an unwritten rule,
there is only ever one per team.

SKILLS: ★ ★ ★

In general, for the level of amateur tournaments
in Rome, likely to be very strong – but
sometimes naive, and the tricks of the more
expert players can get the better of him.

RISK TO (YOUR) KNEES: ☆ ☆ ☆

Likely to be so focused on himself that
the only way he could hurt someone is
by accidentally running into them.

FRIEND POTENTIAL: ☆ ☆ ☆

If you know one, you avoid him.

Almost always in his twenties, more serious
than his mates, he feels like a professional and
dresses like a professional, with an undercut and
side-parting like Cristiano Ronaldo or bleached
hair like Lorenzo Insigne. Wears boots without
laces that he pulls on like flippers. His socks
are pulled right up to the knee unless his shins
are tattooed, in which case socks are kept low
like Totti so the tattoos can be seen. The more
exacting players wax their legs and tuck their
shirts into high-waist shorts, and obviously the
three pieces of kit have to match: all Real Madrid
or all Bayern Munich, only the top teams. In a
tournament he will naturally
assume the captaincy,
sporting an arm band and
showing a deep respect for
the ref. When it comes
to taking a free kick,
he stands with his feet
wide apart and takes
a deep breath before
starting his run-up.

The Eccentric

RARITY: ★ ★ ★

You see few of them in a city
as conformist as Rome.

SKILLS: ★ ☆ ☆

Eccentricity often reflects
a lack of professionalism.

RISK TO (YOUR) KNEES: ☆ ☆ ☆

A pacifist – usually.

FRIEND POTENTIAL: ★ ★ ★

Likely to be someone who travels a lot and
has many interests outside football.

Wearing a David Foster Wallace bandana and
the Thai national team shirt bought on holiday, a
kit from an African outfit or one from the 1980s
bought on eBay, the eccentric is careful to stand
out, even on the football pitch. His game is
never boring either. Passing the ball just a few
metres is a conformist humiliation; better to
hoof it to the player furthest away or shoot from
midfield. He chats during the game and even
manages to laugh, taking everything lightly.
Style is always the priority, even over winning.

A Sign of the Times

SARAH GAINSFORTH
Translated by Alan Thawley

Mario is a slightly scary-looking giant of man. The skin of his face has been baked by the sun and he has a cross tattooed on his forehead. For hours every day he sits with his legs wide apart, always in the same spot outside the San Michele a Ripa Grande complex, on a step at the entrance to one of the ground-floor workshops that have been closed for many years now. The 334-metre-long building was built in several stages from the late 17th century to cater for the city's poor, on a site beside the Tiber, which at that point separates the *rioni* (the historic districts of central Rome) of Testaccio and Trastevere. It started life as a hospice and orphanage and later also became a prison housing women and minors at a time when the Church took responsibility for the care and containment of those the city feared, its poor and its outcasts. Inside the complex, numerous workshops, including a woollen mill, offered young people the opportunity to learn a trade.

Cars come to a stop at the traffic lights then move off again. Mario seems to be busy washing something in the nearby fountain, known as the Fontana del Timone because of its ship's-wheel (*timone*) design. It was one of the nine built in Rome in the 1930s, one per *rione*, in this case the Rione Ripa, which coincides

184 THE PASSENGER Rome

with the Aventine Hill. I ask Mario what it is he's washing. 'I'm washing the fountain,' he replies good naturedly, then tells me about himself.

Rome has always been full of poor people, beggars and the mentally ill. People who inhabit its nooks, crannies, stairways and streetscapes, who merge into these places and ultimately become a feature of them. Like the lady who lived in a corner of the square containing the Arch of Janus before it was gated off. Locals said she had once been a teacher but had at some point – no one knows why – lost her mind. Quiet and reserved, she was accepted by everyone as a slightly unusual presence. All her belongings, including numerous books, were piled up beneath a large plastic sheet, tethered in place with a few ropes. She would come and go, her extremely long hair grown into a tangled mass. Once, when she was gone for a few hours, some tourists decided to poke around in her gear. She flew into a rage, and the neighbourhood stood up for her.

Thirty years ago, according to the Church charity Caritas Roma, there were just three thousand people of no fixed abode in the capital. According to recent estimates, up to fourteen thousand now live in the hidden corners of the city, in shacks or in shelters that they are unable to leave for lack of any alternative. Over the years services and help for the homeless have improved, but poverty has increased, changed, and it now affects more people. At the same time, warns Bishop Benoni Ambarus, the director of Caritas, the city is fragmented and self-absorbed, at risk of becoming a non-community.

On the map of short-term tourist lets you can clearly see a forest of red dots – each of them indicating an unoccupied home – marking out the banks of the Tiber. Some complain that Rome is losing its soul because the historic centre is home to fewer and fewer residents and more and more tourists. In the meantime, along the banks of the river, below street level, the city of the invisible has sprung up. The inhabitants of the riverside are rarely seen, but sometimes you hear them talking, see them fishing or catch a whiff of their cooking or their refuse. By night they sleep in tin and cardboard shacks; by day they scale the banks, suddenly emerge from the vegetation, jump over the parapet and join the inhabitants of the city above. Every so often the police destroy their homes, leaving the tin, wood and cardboard behind. It takes the plants more than a year to cover over the remains of these demolished shacks, hiding them from view.

Behind the vegetation, opposite the San Michele complex, on the other bank of the Tiber, a young man gets ready to go to work. He dresses, attaches a large delivery bag to his bike, climbs up the riverbank, hops over the parapet and slips swiftly into the Lungotevere traffic. Mario carries on washing the fountain. He likes the smell of cleanliness, he tells me. As I say goodbye I think how the city has changed. But perhaps, seen from here, it hasn't really changed all that much.

An Author Recommends

A book, a film and an album to understand Rome, chosen by:

NADIA TERRANOVA
Translated by Alan Thawley

Nadia Terranova is originally from Messina, but she now lives in Rome, where many of her stories are set, including those published in her collection *Come una storia d'amore* (Giulio Perrone Editore, 2020). Her novel *Gli anni al contrario* (Einaudi, 2015) won numerous awards including the Bagutta Prize for a debut novel. *Farewell, Ghosts* (Seven Stories, 2020) is her first novel to be translated into English and was a finalist for the Strega Prize in Italy. She has also written books for younger readers, including *Bruno: Il bambino che imparò a volare* (Orecchio Acerbo, 2012), *Casca il mondo* (Mondadori, 2016) and *Omero è stato qui* (Bompiani, 2019, selected for the Strega children's award). Her books have been published in translation all around the world. She contributes to various publications and online journals, including *La Repubblica*, *Il Foglio*, *Tuttolibri* and *Linkiesta*.

THE BOOK
BUIO IN SALA: GUIDA BREVE AI CINEMA DI ROMA ('Lights Out in the Auditorium: A Brief Guide to the Cinemas of Rome')
Stefano Scanu (Giulio Perrone Editore, 2016)

In the hottest summer of recent years, following the closure of twenty-eight cinemas, Stefano Scanu took to exploring Rome by scooter to create a sentimental map of the city's movie houses. This is, in itself, a filmic image: a writer and bookseller, a latter-day Nanni Moretti, wandering, wraith-like, in search of his own Spoon River, searching for the lost cinemas, those that remain, those that resist, those that have transformed themselves or been transformed to survive, those that have changed or remained true to their spirit, fading away or rejuvenating. He wanted to capture the moment, and the result is twofold: first, an entertaining personal diary, both moving and ironic, in which Scanu has recorded *his* Rome and *his* perspective on the seventh art; second, a fascinating guide for anyone searching for the city beyond the clichés. There is a well-known connection between the cinema and Rome, but behind the huge, emblematic façade (Fellini, Sordi, Cinecittà) there is a quieter daily dialogue between those who live here and the cinemas they visit, from film clubs to multiplexes and everything in between. I read this book while mentally creating an alternative based on my own itineraries, and I feel it is a story that might never end. Rooted in their neighbourhoods or beacons for visitors, Rome's cinemas have myriad stories to tell; getting to know the city through them is one way to avoid experiencing it simply as a tourist.

THE FILM
BIMBA COL PUGNO CHIUSO
('Girl With the Raised Fist')
Claudio Di Mambro, Luca Mandrile
and Umberto Migliaccio (2013)

Giovanna Marturano, a partisan in the Garibaldi Brigade, was born in Rome in 1912 and died there at the age of 101. She was awarded a medal for military valour, was a Knight Grand Cross of the Order of Merit of the Italian Republic and honorary president of the Roman branch of the National Association of Italian Partisans. As a child she helped her family with their resistance activities, and at the age of twenty-six she became a clandestine member of the Communist Party. In Rome she studied at the Liceo Visconti then enrolled as an architecture student but had to interrupt her university career to move to Milan, where she worked in a factory. She was arrested and then released but was labelled as a 'subversive'. In 1941 she defiantly visited the prison island of Ventotene (where her mother was imprisoned) to marry Pietro Grifone, a fellow partisan and future Communist Party MP, whom she had met when she was at school. Throughout her life Marturano devoted herself to politics, the rights of the oppressed and sharing her experiences as a partisan. Back in the days when she used to prepare and distribute fliers she was nicknamed the 'girl with the raised fist', hence the title of this fine documentary. I discovered it in one of those cinemas where you can still find something other than the most predictable fare. On my way out I bought the DVD, which I keep as a talisman. The film explores Rome but also contextualises it within a wider Italian geography – avoiding the easy trap of seeing the capital in isolation – and it condenses a century of Italian history into the biography of one extraordinary woman.

THE ALBUM
COME L'ORO ('Like Gold')
Giulia Anania (2017)

When she sings, Rome is a woman: my mind is filled with the voice, tousled beauty and poignant irony of Gabriella Ferri when I'm travelling through the city, by the Tiber or the Aniene, whether I feel melancholy or electrified with the sensation that only this city can produce. For nearly twenty years I have lived here and for nearly twenty years, albeit always slightly off-key, I have been singing to myself in a slightly dumb euphoria that tastes like water without salt. For the past few years Gabriella Ferri has been joined by another voice, that of Giulia Anania. She is a talented young singer-songwriter who sings of the eastern outskirts of the city without complacency, the colours 'of gold and dust', the working-class and lower-middle-class lives. In her lyrics and videos, Anania can turn a builder's scaffolding into something majestic, portraying the workman himself as a pagan god looking down on the city from above ('I believe in lime / I believe that people are just strange trajectories'), an urban landscape in which humans are just a detail. Giulia Anania's Rome is, appropriately, more reminiscent of Mumbai than New York or London and is certainly not interested in being compared with Milan. It withdraws to the edges and contracts, expanding like a vast border. In *Come l'oro* the songs alternate with 'poems on the phone', verse stories in Roman dialect, in which love is a distrusted presence, men are layabouts and women have grown used to not being able to count on them. And if one relationship ends and another begins between the tables of Pigneto, amid old wounds (so familiar 'I even took them as lovers') and voices like wind on hearts of leaves, we all have 'hearts like a patched-up Chinese vase'.

The Playlist

GIULIA CAVALIERE
Translated by Alan Thawley

You can listen to this playlist at:
open.spotify.com/user/iperborea

Rome is her diehards, those who live there and couldn't live elsewhere, who can talk of nothing else, who would take the Trullo neighbourhood in summertime over a *trullo* holiday home in Puglia, those who can't take it any more, who have had enough of the city but just can't let her go, those who always stand there trying to make up their minds as they miss their bus when it passes, Rome the Eternal City, eternally lagging behind her historical head-start – cradle, bowels, aspiration and grave; Rome, if I didn't go, I'd wish I had, and if I did go, why on earth did I do that? Rome is her terraces and grand hotels, glories past and inglorious present. *Roma amoR*, the opposite of love. Rome is her language, embraced with swagger and passion in traditional songs, an object of pity in disorderly lines, 'Roma nuda', Franco Califano's naked city made flesh, transformed in the wee small hours into his confidante, a mother, a goddess. Rome past and present, tradition artfully remixed. Rome sings of her Madonnas, the Madonna of the angels and the Madonna 'dell'Urione', Rome is Ottorino Respighi's city of fountains and pine trees, from the Via Appia Antica to Valle Giulia, on to the Janiculum and back again. Rome out to have fun, full of contradictions, Folkstudio and rap, Il Locale and trap; Rome allowing herself – on occasion – to be embraced by an outsider passing through, an occasional Roman, who nonetheless understood, opened treasure chests, stole her heart: Rome of miracles. Rome is her tourists, her Japanese visitors, her Vespas – they don't even make them like that any more – Rome bemoaning the present, harking back to fathers' memories, melting on the *sampietrini* and dreaming of dips in the Fontanone, Red Rome hit by bombs in San Lorenzo, spoiled, chemical Rome in Corso Trieste.

Rome the reflection of all confusion. *Dolce Vita* gone, Rome tired and lost, lover and beloved; Rome in the frontline, dirty, dazed, all wedding favour and whipped cream. Rome making music and inspiring music, never missing a beat, creating harmony and ripping it up, Rome who will never be told but is catalogued, immortalised in song, cursed in melody.

1

Ottorino
Respighi
*La fontana
di Valle Giulia
all'alba*

2

Colle der
Fomento
*Il cielo
su Roma*

3

Franco
Califano
Roma nuda

4

Carl Brave /
Franco126
Solo guai

5

Matia Bazar
*Vacanze
romane*

6

Lucio Dalla
*La sera
dei miracoli*

7

Ardecore
*Madonna
de l'Urione*

8

Francesco
De Gregori
San Lorenzo

9

Momus
*Giapponese
a Roma*

10

Virginiana
Miller
*L'eternità
di Roma*

11

I Cani
Corso Trieste

12

Remo
Remotti
*Mamma Roma
addio!*

Digging Deeper

READING

Edoardo Albinati
The Catholic School
Farrar, Straus and Giroux, 2019 (USA)
/ Picador, 2020 (UK)

Giancarlo De Cataldo
Romanzo Criminale
Atlantic, 2015

Claudia Durastanti
Cleopatra Goes to Prison
Dedalus, 2020

Carlo Emilio Gadda
That Awful Mess on the Via Merulana
New York Review of Books, 2007

Amara Lakhous
*Clash of Civilizations Over
an Elevator in Piazza Vittorio*
Europa Editions, 2008

Keti Lelo, Salvatore Monni
and Federico Tomassi
Le mappe della disuguaglianza
Donzelli, 2019

Elsa Morante
History: A Novel
Steerforth, 2000

Gianluigi Nuzzi
*Ratzinger Was Afraid: The Secret
Documents, the Money and the Scandals
that Overwhelmed the Pope* (ebook)
Casaleggio Associati, 2013

Francesco Pacifico
The Story of My Purity
Farrar, Straus and Giroux, 2013

Pier Paolo Pasolini
The Street Kids
Europa Editions, 2016

Emanuele Trevi
Something Written
World Editions, 2016

Various authors (edited by Chiara
Stangalino and Maxim Jakubowski)
Rome Noir
Akashic, 2009

Various authors (edited by Helen Constantine)
Rome Tales
Oxford University Press, 2011

Sandro Veronesi
The Hummingbird
Weidenfeld and Nicolson, 2021

WATCHING

Ludovico Bessegato, Ludovico Di Martino
Skam Italia
2018–20

Claudio Caligari
Don't Be Bad (*Non essere cattivo*)
2015

Claudio Canepari, Giuseppe Ghinami
I mille giorni di Mafia Capitale
2017

Andrea De Sica, Anna Negri,
Letizia Lamartire
Baby
2018–20

Damiano and Fabio D'Innocenzo
Bad Tales (Favolacce)
2020

Federico Fellini
La Dolce Vita
1960

Matteo Garrone
Dogman
2018

Nanni Moretti
Dear Diary (Caro diario)
1993

Ferzan Özpetek
A Perfect Day (Un giorno perfetto)
2008

Gianfranco Rosi
Sacro GRA
2013

Andrea Segre
Magari le cose cambiano
2009

Paolo Sorrentino
The Great Beauty (La grande bellezza)
2013

Paolo Sorrentino
The Young Pope
2016

William Wyler
Roman Holiday
1953

Graphic design and art direction: Tomo Tomo and Pietro Buffa

Photography: Andrea Boccalini

Photographic content curated by Prospekt Photographers

Illustrations: Francesca Arena

Infographics and cartography: Pietro Buffa

Managing editor (English-language edition): Simon Smith

Thanks to: Magda Andreola, Rosaria Carpinelli, Mattia Carratello, Marco Cassini, Maddalena Cazzaniga, Cesare from the *Anaconda*, Danno, Guido Gazzaniga, Nicola Lagioia, Giona Lodigiani, Tiziana Lo Porto, Lorenzo Margaglio and Michele from La Mirage Sporting Club, Ilaria Mieli, Matteo Nucci, Paolo the Eco-Warrior, Rocco Piovani, Christian Raimo, Pablo Riccomi, Martina Testa

The opinions expressed in this publication are those of the authors and do not purport to reflect the views and opinions of the publishers.

http://europaeditions.com/thepassenger
http://europaeditions.co.uk/thepassenger
#ThePassengerMag

Translators: Lucy Rand (Revolutions in the Suburbs, What We Talk About When We Talk About *Calciotto*, Portraits of *Calciotto* Players), Will Schutt (Rome Does Not Judge), Oonagh Stransky (The Not So Eternal City, Roman Soundscapes, The Soul of the City, 39 Notes for a Book on Rome, Ambitionz as a Roman: Trap from Trastevere, sidebars, picture captions), Alan Thawley (The Echo of the Fall, Recent Mayors of Rome, A Sign of the Times, An Author Recommends, The Playlist, sidebars, editorial, photographer's biography, standfirsts, picture captions), Deborah Wassertzug (The Family)

ISBN 9781787703544

Printed on Munken Pure thanks to the support of Arctic Paper
Printed by ELCOGRAF S.p.A., Verona, Italy